FINDING HIS FAVOR IN YOUR
WILDERNESS

Finding His Favor In Your

WILDERNESS

Receiving the favor of God in the dismal,
dry unproductive areas of your life

Dr. Herldleen Russell

XULON PRESS

Xulon Press
2301 Lucien Way #415
Maitland, FL 32751
407.339.4217
www.xulonpress.com

Printed in the United States of America.

ISBN-13: 978-1-6628-0358-1

ACKNOWLEDGEMENT

T he author alone writes no book. There are times God allows life circumstances to impregnate individuals to give birth in writing their experiences to share with others. Along the way others make contributions, some good and some bad to produce a vehicle to help others in their life's journey.

My life long friend Glenda Love High, who takes up the long tedious task each time to edit the manuscript. Tawanda Davis who administrates the process, gently shoving me to meet the deadlines.

DEDICATION

My family. always my inspiration that exceeds biologically now including 18 grand children and five great grand children. To my family that extends spiritually all over the world and have been contributing factors help birth this book. *I have found His Favor in My Wilderness.*

To my Lord and Savior Jesus Christ. It is in Him I move and have my being and without Him I can do nothing.

> *This is what the Lord says The people who survive the sword will find favor in the wilderness; I will come to give rest," The Lord appeared to us in the past, saying: I have loved you with an everlasting love; I have drawn you with unfailing kindness. I will build you up again, and you, will be rebuilt (Jeremiah 31:1-4)*

TABLE OF CONTENTS

Introduction xi

Chapter 1: What is a Wilderness? 1

Chapter 2: Let's make it Personal. 12

Chapter 3: God Supplies 22

Chapter 4: My Wilderness Purpose sets
            me Apart 40

Chapter 5: That Wonderful Grace
            in the Wilderness 48

Chapter 6: Lessons From the Potter's House . . . 55

Chapter 7: The Who verses The What? 62

Chapter 8: I will Grow and Mature
            in my Wilderness 82

Chapter 9: The Corridors of Faith. 88

Chapter 10: When you *Think* your Wilderness
is the End of it all —
Final Destination. 94

Chapter 11: In Your Wilderness You can bloom
where you have been planted. 99

Chapter 12: Growing in Grace 119

Chapter 13: Learning How to Operate
in God's Timing 133

Chapter 14: When Grace has been lifted 139

Chapter 15: The Dead End that is ....Destiny
Waiting to Happen 150

Chapter 16: That Marvelous Favor of God 161

INTRODUCTION

"Thus saith the LORD, The people which were left of the sword found grace in the wilderness; even Israel, when I went to cause him to rest" (Jeremiah 31:2).

My first invitation to Uganda, East Africa was to speak at a Women's Conference. I stayed in the Pastor and his family's home. His wife's name was Grace, which is not to me a usual African name, so I asked her how did she receive it. She told me the following story.

It happened during the time of the notorious dictator, Edi Amin's reign. It was a horrible, grievous, desolate and fearful time for that country. History records the reign of terror that he had. Grace's father was in his army. Her father and mother had two girls, or as her father said, "She gave me two girls." When the mother got pregnant again, he warned her that if she brought another girl home, she would be in trouble. He was a very abusive man. By the time of the birth, the father had done something to displease Edi Amin and had been thrown into prison. When the baby was born, and it was another girl, the mother named her *Grace*. Her reasoning was because God looked on her and gave her His favor, grace in this terrible, hopeless time in her life...*grace in her wilderness.* Isn't it interesting how she perceived it? Not discouraged. "Another girl! What's the use? My husband is going to... How could God do this again, knowing my situation?"

Look at her perspective.

Your situation may not be that dire or dramatic, but we all experience wildernesses in our lives. Yours may be the isolation of a life which often feels frenzied and hectic as you hurry from one appointment to the next, returning phone calls and checking items off your seemingly infinite to-do list. We mount a treadmill of repetitive duties. Sometimes collapsing in sheer mental or physical exhaustion, we will question and wonder, "Is this what God has for my life?" It's a dark, unproductive, unfulfilling place. How do I get off this treadmill? How can I even take the time to see what direction God wants me to move in my life? What if He wants to make changes? All that alone can be a little frightening, especially if I am in a comfort zone. Then what appears to happen is my emotional environment becomes a *wilderness*-a dry, dismal point. But there *is* purpose, I have found, whereby He can speak to me.

Frustrating your process to achieve His purpose.

When I was working at my computer from the very early morning, my sight started getting a little blurred, but I kept pressing because of the many deadlines I had to reach. After I really couldn't focus too much, I finally got up just to walk away to the family room to prop my feet up, getting away from my office. When I got to the family room, which is adjacent to the sunroom, I noticed the rays of the sun streaming through the windows. They were beckoning me on this chilly fall morning.

I walked past the pile of clothes that needed to be folded on the couch in the family room. Moving into the sunroom, I sat on the couch in there as the warm rays flooded over me, feeling the warmth and resting. I realized that the Lord had called me away from the day's overwhelming deadlines, cluttered office and household chores so thereby He could speak to me. It was Grace enveloping me in my personal wilderness so that the S-O-N could shine, flood me with His warmth, and tell me something that I was too busy previously to hear.

> *"...grace in the wilderness...when I went to cause [her] to rest" (v. 2).*

As believers, we readily attribute our salvation to God's grace, but what does this grace, which we trust God to give, mean to us? We need to be reminded that it is a benefit promised to us not just at salvation: "By grace are [you] saved" (Ephesians 2:8 KJV), but throughout our walk with the Lord.

> *"Therefore, having been justified by faith, we have peace with God through our*

*Lord Jesus Christ, through whom also
we have access by faith into this grace
in which we stand, and rejoice in hope of
the glory of God"* (Romans 5:1-2).

How does it work out in everyday life, especially
when we're going through periods of trial or suffering in our own personal wilderness? In the passage of Scripture written by the prophet, Jeremiah
as referred to earlier, the first word that caught my
attention was *wilderness*. Even though the word is
not something anyone desires, in the same verse,
the sound of promise just rings out. It's a wilderness...**but** we will find grace, the unmerited favor of
God. Grace in the midst of the wilderness--some-
thing that is totally different from that environment.

Historically, in this passage, the prophet is writing
a letter, a *Word from the Lord*, to God's chosen
people that were exiled after their captivity. A false
prophet had spoken lies to them concerning this
time of exile. God had to correct the untruth that
had the people turn their focus from Him onto those
false promises. Jeremiah, God's chosen prophet and

intercessor for the people, seeks God about what was happening.

> *He alone is God who can never be sought*
> *in vain; not even when he cannot be*
> *found.— Bernard Clairvaux (Clairvaux),*
> *Saint Bernard On Consideration – Saint*
> *Bernard (of Clairvaux) 1908)*

God speaks—to tell His people the truth. Even though physically, they were left in the wilderness, they were not alone. There was **grace**, and in the midst of this tragedy, God gave them **rest**. There would be a time of restoration from captivity and healing of their wounds resulting from it. It was all for purpose, though they could not see it at the time. It would be a *wilderness*—but a *rest*, whereby He could speak to them. Do you hear the good news in that? It's really **great** news and a powerful truth.

What is this truth He is going to speak to you whenever you're going through a difficult time? We just need to settle ourselves, receive the rest that He alone can give, open our ears, and say as the young boy, Samuel: "Speak [Lord], for your servant hears" (1 Samuel 3:10).

Refer to 1Samuel 3. The entire chapter records one of Israel's darkest times in history. God had not spoken to His people, and prophetic visions were not often. The people did not have access to the Bible as we do; therefore, they waited to hear *a word from the Lord* through the priest and or the prophets.

The leadership at this time had fallen into sin, and God was not speaking as before, and when He did, it was very rare. When you are in a place that you should not be, God's message is always to stop, repent. It does not have to be sin as we define it, but when we are out of the will of God, disobedience is still sin. He may not speak often at this time, but His love always gives us a chance, and He will speak, but the message is still the same: **Turn from sin and come back into relationship with Him**. He does not want a partial obedience that suits you, to receive His blessings; He wants a life committed.

And history records the faithfulness and unconditional love of their God in spite of their sin. Time after time, He would faithfully raise up someone that wanted to hear and serve Him, and they would then speak the truth to His people. This time it was a young boy named Samuel.

Samuel's mother was Hannah, who was previously barren (not able to have children). She prayed and promised the Lord that if He would give her a son, she would, indeed, give him back to Him. God answered her prayer, and she kept her promise. Samuel lived in the temple under the tutelage of Eli, the priest at that time. However, Eli had not kept the commands of God and also allowed his sons to desecrate the Temple.

Now, you can understand why in those days the word of the Lord was rare. The priest went about his temple duties as a religious ritual, but there is no substance if God is not in it or speaking. It became just a duty, as any life would be if there was no relationship involved, if there was no direction from the Director of your life.

How personal and the degree of intimacy in relationships always make the difference in good communication.

Sin had broken this relationship, and the priest's life and service had become just a religious duty, without any expectation to hear from the Lord. God desires relationship with His people, and we are made for relationship. That's why He sent His only Son, Jesus, into the world to reconcile us back to Him, to reestablish that personal relationship.

> *"Long ago God spoke to the fathers by the prophets at different times and in different ways. In these last days, He has spoken to us by His Son" (Hebrews 1:1 HCSB).*

Back to Samuel. God faithfully raises up a prophet so He can, again, have a spokesperson to communicate His heart. One night while young Samuel was asleep, he hears someone call his name. It was the voice of God, but, sad to say, Samuel had not ever heard or experienced the Lord because he was living in that season when God's Word was so rare. Therefore, he did not recognize the voice of the Lord when He spoke.

A thoughtful challenge.

How are we raising up our next generation to hear or to know what is right if we don't know His voice, the Word of God? If we know and are not the examples of what a personal relationship can be, what effect will that have on them? Personal relationship, of course, includes personal communication.

Consequently, when Samuel heard a distinct voice calling him, he did not recognize it was the Lord's voice speaking to him. So, he goes to the only contact that he knows, Eli. The record says when Samuel heard this voice in the night, he immediately went to his mentor, Eli, three times and said, "Here I am." But each time, Eli said to him, "I did not call [you]." Eli, finally recognizing the reality of the situation, says to Samuel, "The next time you hear the voice, say, 'Speak, Lord, Your servant hears.'" (See 1 Samuel 3:4-9.)

God desires to speak to us in the difficult times, in our midnight seasons, in our wilderness. He can allow circumstances whereby they will make us stop so we can hear what He has to say to us personally. This could be what your wilderness is all about. And understanding this truth will help us as we inevitably walk through tough times. In times of suffering, our question is usually some version of "Why is God allowing this?" That's a fair question, and it's okay to ask. I've asked that before, and, no doubt, will again. But I have found that a better question to ask is "Could this be a midnight moment, a season in which God wants to teach me something about Himself? About me?" *Speak, Lord!*

> **So, I ask you, as you read this book, to ask the Lord to open your spiritual ears and your heart to hear what He wants to say to you...**

It is not just *grace in the wilderness*. What I found out is not only is that a *sufficient* grace, as the Apostle Paul said in his testimony, but it's grace that is *more than enough*. (See 2 Corinthians 12:7-9.). As you journey with me through the following chapters, my desire is that you can identify and navigate your personal wildness into your promise destiny and experience His favor every step of the way.

CHAPTER 1

WHAT IS A WILDERNESS?

A wilderness is a place of very little growth, if any. It's a place of loneliness, no potential or possibilities.

When you are traveling and you arrive at a wilderness, it's a place you want to go *through* to get to your desired destination—not even pause, stay for any length of time, and certainly not set up residence. It's the ghost towns of life. A wilderness is a place I want to **get out of**, geographically, emotionally, and physically.

It is not the Where we are— It's the How we go through!

How we journey through unexpected circumstances produces the learning experience that the

1

Lord wants us to be partakers of. It depends on what we believe about the road we're on. If familiar with the Psalms 42:5 (KJV) Scripture, we tell ourselves what to do using words of the psalmist, "Hope thou in God." We say these words repeatedly as if it is a mantra.

For me, there were three powerful phrases of encouragement as I began my journey *in* and *through* my wilderness. The words are what I heard over and over, a still small voice whispering again and again:

"Can you trust Me?"

"Do you trust Me!"

"Can you trust Me" NOW in this place, this situation, this environment?

I had no immediate answer. I then looked at myself and began to question, examining myself, asking, "What have I done to end up at this place?" The focus is on me, initially. Self-examination is always good, but I have to take my eyes off of the *emotional me* because it can easily become a *pity party*.

Need to refocus.

How? By fixing our eyes on the truth about our journey and remember the One who sets our course.

Ruth Chou Simmons words: "You can find hope in the present when you face and preach the truth to yourself about where you're headed." Ruth Chou Simons on an article written by her called *Staying the Course* (July, 2018, Encouragement for Today).

The wilderness is never meant to be a place of residence, though sometimes it appears that we have been in this place longer than we have not. I remembered it took the Israelites 40 years to go through their wilderness before they reached their promised land. Why so long? Because while traveling, they consistently questioned and disobeyed God; yet, God was still forgiving and took them *through*. Their wilderness travel that should have taken about 11 days took 40 years!

Which brings us back to the **How** you go through your wilderness, which is of vast importance. God spoke through His servants giving them instructions each step, but they chose to disobey Him. Their disobedience, the *how*, prolonged their time in the wilderness.

It's really that simple; we need only to look to God's Word, which is "a lamp unto [our] feet, and a light unto [our] path" (Psalms 119:105 KJV). A lamp shows us where we are, and the light guides us to where we need to go. We should have goals and objectives, and when we fix our eyes daily on the eternal hope of Jesus, the Living Word, and speak the truth of the Word to ourselves, we will begin to see that no present obstacle or any situation is ever bigger than He—even in this horrible wilderness.

What is a Wilderness Experience?

Wilderness experiences, to sum up simply, are the trials that you go through in your life. The trial can be defined as a dry period of your life that is unproductive without help because the entire environment is not conducive to growth, support or help. What makes it a wilderness is isolation for you. People can even surround you; yet, in a wilderness, you are all alone. Your emotions start speaking to you: *Does anyone even care that I am in this place?* The world goes by, and you are stuck in that state of being.

*The Wilderness is **loneliness'** birthing place.*

Spending any length of time in that isolated place, you feel the conception and birth pains of loneliness, let down, feeling sorry for yourself, and its growth rate is uncontrollable—if we allow it.

You are not alone. It is so sad to say that loneliness is a worldwide epidemic. There was a research study that found loneliness and social isolation were both associated with a risk of early death that is on par with that caused by smoking 15 cigarettes a day and exceeds the risk of early death from obesity. An insurance company affirmed that loneliness in America has reached epidemic levels, based on a survey of more than 20,000 American adults.

*The wilderness can be a **loveless** place.*

Loneliness starts, and then the very next emotional feeling is that no one cares. No one loves me. If they loved me, they would show their concern and help me at this time.

The Israelites wondered at this time if their trials meant God no longer loved them. But in Jeremiah

31:3, the prophet reminds them of what God said in the past: "I have loved you with an everlasting love." Everlasting love never stops, and greater than that—it's unconditional. Nothing, absolutely nothing, can separate you from His love. (See Rom. 8:35-39.). Never, ever doubt God's love for you even when you don't feel like He does.

Alone during this time?

Remember, God cares. He knows that you are there. He *allowed* this, and He promises to be there with you. You are not alone. He is right there to supply whatever you need and loving you every step of the way. Never believe the lies of *never*: "I'll *never* survive, I'll *never* prosper, I'll *never* succeed, I'll *never* get the things I desire." Those are the words resulting when the focus is on *you* as you listen to the enemy of our soul. Change your focus, and remember what Jesus said: "I will never leave you nor forsake you" (Hebrews 13:5). Not focusing on *what* but **Who** you need a Word from the **Who.** One word from the Lord is more powerful than a million lies from Satan.

In the wilderness' darkness... a light shines.

It is really interesting that when you are in a dark place how large the place seems. It is implied because you cannot see any boundaries. Darkness can go on and on almost infinitely in your mind. Depending on how long you are in that place, that darkness can soon become overwhelming.

Fear always results when anything overwhelms you. Always looming is the fear of what can happen when something is bigger than you. It's time to face those fears with your God—if you know Him who is light. As you know one small candle lit in a dark place eliminates the darkness.

*Know there is **someone** (not **something**) always bigger than your problem or situation.*

First Kings 20th chapter records the story of a battle of the Israelite army. In this battle, they were outnumbered by their enemy, the Syrians. The battle took place in the hills, and though they were outnumbered, they defeated their enemy because the record shows God was with them.

Eastern cultures, at that time, believed in many gods, idols, and spirits, and those deities were localized. They surmised that the Israelites' God was in the hills, and that is why they were being defeated. Therefore, the enemy's strategy was to fight them, not in the hills, but in the plains.

How large was this enemy army? In comparison, it was said that God's people were like "two little flocks of goats" while their enemy's army "filled the countryside" (v. 27). It was easy to see the darkness in this situation because their eyes were on the place, the situation, and the largeness of their enemy filling the countryside. There were no boundaries as far as the eye could see. They were definitely in a wilderness.

> *No matter how large the place, how overwhelming the situation becomes and how dark it is, it's never bigger than your God.*

Physically, when you are in a dark place, when just the smallest light is turned on, even a candle is lit, the place becomes limited in its size and effect. The light made boundaries to the vast darkness... Such was the case for the Israelites. They knew their God, and a Word from Him would shine the light on the situation and give them directions for this battle. David, the great warrior, reminds us again, "Thy Word is a lamp unto my feet, and a light unto my path" (Psalms119:105 KJV).

God sent a man to the King of Israel and gave them a Word from their God: 'Because the Syrians have said, "The Lord is God of the hills, but He is not God of the valleys," therefore I will deliver all this great multitude into your hand, and you shall know that I am the Lord'" (1 Kings 20:28).

When you are in your wilderness, never leave the Lord God out of it. He was with you on your mountain top experiences when you were happy and everything was going well. He will certainly be with you in your wilderness experiences when everything seems dark and you can't see your way. When the enemy of your soul is overwhelming you, what is the Lord saying about it? Jesus is Lord, Lord over all and every circumstance, when He is lord over your life. It is time to do what He reminds us to: "Call to Me, and I will answer you, and show you great and mighty things" (Jeremiah 33:3).

He still dispels darkness, and there is no darkness that is too dark for His light to shine through and expel.

Now, the Israelite army and the Syrian army camped opposite of each other for seven days. Can you imagine the scene of seeing your enemy, who vastly outnumbers you, facing you for seven days? But God had promised, and what a great thought as I remember... seven is God's number of completion.

Wow, the battle had not even started, but for God, it was completed. You think logistically with your finite mind, but God is bigger. He is the infinite God who knows the ending from the beginning. (See Isaiah 46:10.) You were chosen "before the foundation of the world" (Ephesians 1:4). Before you had a problem, He already had the answer. He knows your problems before they happen, allows them, has the answer and already proclaimed victory, just as He did for the Israelite army.

It makes it exciting to read on to see what happened to their enemy. The seventh day when the battle was drawing, the Israelites fought, and 100,000 footmen were destroyed in one day, and the rest of the army of their enemy ran away into another city where a wall fell on 27,000 of them. (See 1 Kings 20:29-30) God's people were victorious. God proved Himself to be the God of the hills, as well as the plains, to them and all of their enemies. Is He not Creator God that made the hills and the plains? We serve an awesome God.

He saw your wilderness before you entered into it—the hills and the valleys—and already proclaimed that it would work together for your good. (See Romans 8:28). Because, He overcame every situation, challenge and problem in life, when we belong to him we too are overcomers.

CHAPTER 2

LET'S MAKE IT PERSONAL

*What are **you** experiencing in **your** wilderness?*

The wilderness can be as varied as each person. Yours may not be mine, and mine, not yours...but it is realer to you than anyone can understand.

*The Wilderness of **Widowhood or Divorce or...***

Is there ever a lonelier place?

This was at the top of my list, but I'm sure you have one that tops mine. What is at the top of your list is usually what is currently happening to you.

After 47 years of marriage, I became a widow. For some, it could be divorce, or separation from someone or something dear to you—the ending of a relationship. However, for whatever the reason, it's a place where someone has been snatched out of your life, and you are left feeling void and empty to go through a grief process that no one really understands.

I could have said immediately paraphrasing Martha, Lazarus' sister: "If Jesus had been here, he wouldn't have died. Why didn't He come? Why wasn't He here when we called for Him? He allowed this to happen." (See John 11)

Extending it to my situation, "If Jesus was really there and really loved me, why would He have taken my husband away? My whole life has changed and I cannot see any good in it."

The hurt, the loneliness, the pain. If I could just take a pill and get over it, how wonderful that would be, eliminating the pain and filling the void quickly. But this wilderness takes time: "Yea, though I *walk through* the valley of the shadow of death, I will [don't have to] fear no evil" (Psalms 23:4 KJV Emphasis mine). I don't have to fear any evil because the One that allowed this is not only going through it with me, but is also filling that void, the vacancy that it leaves.

So be of good courage. He is the good Shepherd who cares for you and will lead and guide you through this wilderness in your life. You are not there to stay.

Sickness in the Wilderness?

Your sickness is chronic. You have prayed, had many to pray for you; yet, nothing has changed. Some days you wonder: "What's the point? Why keep praying? Why do I even keep hoping? Why keep asking the Lord to heal me?"

On other days, it's "I know the Lord is more than able to heal me, but He hasn't—at least, not yet." So, its longevity produces questions, and I start wondering: "Is it really worth it to keep pouring my heart out to Him? to risk feeling vulnerable again, to even hope again?"

There was the account recorded in John 5:2-9 of an invalid man who probably wondered the same things. He had been an invalid for 38 years—for nearly 40 years of his life, and that could have been all his life. This man had been unable to walk or move on his own, and so he spent his time waiting by a pool called Bethesda. Now, he was not alone physically at this place. It was at this pool that a great number of other disabled people would be—the blind, the lame, and the paralyzed. What an environment to be in during your infirmity! The passage goes on to say *why* they were all there.

Occasionally, an angel came, stirred the waters of the pool, and the first person into it after the stirring would be healed. While it seems like a crazy hope—to wait an indefinite amount of time for just the *opportunity* to receive a miracle—but that's what everyone around the pool was doing...Waiting. Hoping. Praying that "today might be my day when the water was stirred and I could be the first one in." Praying for a change, even just a stirring, and just what I needed resulting from it.

But *he was alone*, and I'm sure he experienced all its emotions and even more loneliness compounded by the fact that he did not have anyone to put him in the water. He also experienced no compassion; no one cared to take the time to help him.

However, greater than the sick that surrounded him year after year and his chances of ever being healed getting slimmer and slimmer, Jesus was there. Jesus knew that he had already been in that terrible condition and position for a long time.

Jesus knows right where you are, your problem, condition and position.

Jesus approaches him simply asked him the question, "Do you want to be made well?" (v 6).

The lame man didn't answer the question; he just started telling Jesus WHY he was not well, from the natural point of view. His focus was on the environment of his sickness and the physical solution (someone needs to put him in the water). His focus was not on the "Great Physician" who was standing right there, "a very present help in [the time] of trouble" (Psalms 46:1). The God who sent the angel to stir the water is, in fact, the One who created the angel, the pool, and the water for that purpose. He is the one that is touched with the "feeling of our infirmities" (Hebrews 4:15 KJV). The One that knows exactly how you feel as you go through your sickness or whatever the problem. The One who *is* time, personified and knows and has your appointed time.

That will happen to us sometimes. We start losing our focus because we start thinking of the WHY, blaming someone else, and or looking to someone else for the solution. But be of good courage. God has a time just for you. Many, many people were surrounding the area, but Jesus came to him. He loves you; He knows your condition, your position!

This is a great example of waiting and how Jesus can show up in your wilderness. But I can hear you saying, "The truth is I'm *still* in my wilderness, suffering, no change; and this is a fact. Here is the question of time again... But **How** long?

Jesus knew the man wanted to get well. He also knew how long the man had been there and how long anyone had made an offer to care. Before this divine miracle, I think Jesus' intent was to restore in him a hope that had grown cold. He did this by asking an obvious question.

We can be like that invalid—each of us with places in our lives where hope has withered like the lame mans limbs from lack of use. If we have been in our wilderness for any length of time, it's easy to lose hope. He sees us and compassionately invites us to believe in hope again, to believe in Him. Not just to be healed of a particular sickness. Jesus always does a deeper work in our lives than just solving the immediate problem. In the King James Version, Jesus asks, "Wilt thou be made whole?" He heals the body, the soul and the spirit, the total man or woman. . He is the only one that can make you "whole…" This question is still asked by Jesus, Do you want to be made whole?

Suffering an undeniable part of life but when you know the undeniable Savior.

Though it doesn't make it easier in the moment, it's good to remember that all suffering is *temporary*. Scripture says that we will suffer "a little while" (1 Peter 5:10 NIV) that we suffer only "momentary light affliction" (2 Corinthians 4:17 HCSB), and that our sufferings are only for the "present time" (Romans 8:18 HCSB).

Remember, God will supply whatever I need *during this time*. That is what makes the entire difference in this bare, isolated, lonely, seemingly-never-changing place, as I wait.

There is another *wilderness* caused by our own foolish decisions.

Have you ever entered into something that you know was wrong? You by past the door of choice and blatantly just walking into it. Flesh-that part of you that wants to be satisfied immediately-took over, and you wanted to just *be*. It was your choice, with no other influence except for the enemy of your soul that wants you to lose ground in your spiritual walk, your purpose and destiny. The Holy Spirit convicted you, and even received words of warning perhaps from others. Those warnings spoke loudly against it. But you continued to walk towards it, crossed the threshold and ended up in it. It is here I usually hear, my mother's voice, "no body to blame but your self."

The resulting guilt you experienced hung over your head like a dark dreary storm cloud shutting out every bit of light that there ever was. Following, was the condemnation that flooded over you like a river washes over a bank during a storm. You heard these words over and over: "You knew better and you cannot blame anyone else; it was simply your choice."

You find yourself in a wilderness created by yourself. Nevertheless, it's still a wilderness—a place of loneliness. Separation from God is your wilderness. It's like the prodigal son who left home, now realizing he has ended up in the pigpen surrounded by pigs. He was ready to eat the same food, sinking lower than he ever possibly could.

However, he remembers a father that loves him in spite of himself and the mistakes he has made, just longing for him to return home. The Word is there to remind us: "If we confess our sins, He [our Father] is faithful and just to forgive us of our sins and to cleanse us from all unrighteousness" (1 John 1:9). My choice now is to walk away from that, that I fell into, not remain and wallow in it.\ as a pig wallows in the mud. Repentance means not only having godly sorrow for what you have done but also turning from it and being assured that "there is therefore now no condemnation to those who are in Christ Jesus, who do not walk according to the flesh, but according to the Spirit" (Romans 8:1). When I obey the Word in my wilderness, there comes the cleansing and the experience of His immeasurable grace. Mercy rescues me, and grace gives me that unmerited favor of restoration. "Goodness and mercy... follow me" (Psalms 23:6) with the unconditional love that He gives me. Oh, what a love that's shown in the unmerited favor of God, which is called grace.

CHAPTER 3

GOD SUPPLIES

♫ What ever you need?.....God's got it...
He's got everything you need

L et's look at what Isaiah says God supplies as he addresses Israel, God's people.

Isaiah 32:15-20

*15Until the Spirit is poured upon us
from on high,
And the wilderness becomes a fruitful field,
And the fruitful field is counted as a forest.
16Then justice will dwell in the wilderness,
And righteousness remain in the
fruitful field.
17 The work of righteousness will be peace,*

*And the effect of righteousness, quietness
and assurance forever.*
*18 My people will dwell in a peaceful
habitation,
In secure dwellings, and in quiet
resting places,
19 Though hail comes down on the forest,
And the city is brought low in humiliation.
20 Blessed are you who sow beside
all waters,
Who send out freely the feet of the ox and
the donkey.*

There are a lot of promises in that passage of Scripture, but to understand it fully, let's go back historically to those times in which it was written.

Geographically, rural areas or wildernesses in Bible times were not serene retreats from a complicated urban existence. The countryside was usually short on law and order, so aptly described in Judges 21:25: "Everyone did what was right in his own eyes," for their own protection. And when man operates thusly, history proves the results have never been favorable, ending with nothing but chaos.

Physically, their cities had walls built around them and were the places that offered relative peace and protection—*relative* peace, but never 100% security. But the Lord had made a promise to His people. His promise pledged to protect Jerusalem from their enemy, Assyria, at that time. Isaiah pictured God as an angry bird (see Isaiah 31:5) that dives, pecks, and claws in order to guard its young.

Other analogies are shown in the Psalms. David described himself as resting in "the shadow of [God's] wings" (17:8), and another offers assurance that the Lord would "cover you with His feathers, And under His wings you shall take refuge" (91:4).

How can you see it? Every time you see a bird darting about to protect its nestlings can be a reminder not only of God's care but of His intervention when trouble arises.

My very good friend, Glenda, has a bird that builds a nest, of all places, in between concrete beams in an alcove on her front porch. She has tried many, many things to evict this bird, but to no avail. I won't even list the things she has done that should have worked. But each time after the destruction of the nest, the bird diligently starts over building her nest, and when

Glenda returns home, there again is another nest. This happens year after year. All methods intended to be deterrents seem only to develop more persistence in that bird not to be perturbed, disturbed, distracted, or discouraged in what its mission is.

Does this not remind you of our loving Father, who never sleeps or slumbers? Who is not deterred by the circumstances but consistently builds, shelters, and takes care of you in the greatest, hardest, adverse situation? He makes a home for you in the worst environment, and nothing stops Him. He is a very *present* help and a *presence* in the time of trouble, meeting every need as He looks over His child, providing that dwelling place we need. That reality makes Isaiah's vision of justice in the wilderness quoted at the beginning of this chapter a remarkable promise.

> *It is not the wilderness that the change will be in, but the greatest change will be in me.*

God's presence and our key to transformation, change, would be the presence of His Spirit. (See Isaiah 32:15) God's presence in the wilderness brings also

His attributes. He will speak peace. Understand, God has a process and procedure required of His people in enacting this change. He can transform the place and He does sometimes but that is just geography and can be just temporary. But transforming His people is His greatest desire, so they can endure or see what He wants them to learn in this place, whereby when the places of circumstances again arise, they are equipped to handle them. It is His ultimate endeavor for them to go on and reach their destiny.

A peace that passes all understanding.

I need peace. I long for peace, "for God is not the author of confusion" (1 Corinthians 14:33). I seek Him, the Author, to settle my heart and mind through Jesus Christ. I may not initially understand what is happening, but He brings this peace that passes all understanding. In His presence, I find peace, but not all the time understanding. It is important to know that it is not imposed through force.

Isaiah says the Spirit would not impose God's peace on unwilling people. The peace that they needed would result from their righteous *acts* And His (God's) ways are not our ways.

*They had to be **active** in their wilderness.*

Just as that bird on Glenda's front porch diligently built, no matter what the circumstances were, note that the bird was never discouraged. That mother bird simply kept actively doing what was right to establish an environment of safety and protection for her young.

We don't think of *being active* in the wilderness; rather, just wanting and waiting to get out are our thoughts, at that time. "When I get out, I will be able to continue to carry on with my life." But God's ways are not our ways. The wilderness will afford you opportunity to be an active presence, to do *righteous acts.*

> *After we have perfect relationship with God, through the satisfying work of the Holy Spirit, this faith must be exercised in the realities of everyday life. – O. Chambers*

*The first **action** in your wilderness.*

Isaiah 32:9-13 (HCSB)

⁹Stand up, you complacent women; listen to me. Pay attention to what I say, you overconfident daughters.

¹⁰ In a little more than a year you overconfident ones will shudder, for the vintage will fail and the harvest will not come.

¹¹ Shudder, you complacent ones; tremble, you overconfident ones! Strip yourselves bare and put sackcloth around your waists.

¹² Beat your breasts in mourning for the delightful fields and the fruitful vines,

¹³ for the ground of my people growing thorns and briers, indeed, for every joyous house in the joyful city.

What was the first action commanded?

The Lord instructed Judah's complacent women to wail for the consequences looming over their corrupt society. The wilderness is not a place of complacency, so what do I start doing? Prayer is always the first action. When trouble looms, prayer is always a good first step to take. But having a foundation upon which to build our prayers also makes a difference. It is the One to Whom you direct your prayers that is the Foundation, the One that makes the promise to fulfill what you need.

Talking to and hearing from the One that allows this, has a purpose for it, and can do something about it is what is needed. Relationship is the requirement.

> *You are my friends, if you do what I command you. I do not call you slaves anymore, because a slave doesn't know what his master is doing. I have called you friends, because I have made known to you everything I have heard from My Father... I chose you.*

*I assure you: Anything you ask the Father
in My name, He will give you. Until now
you have asked for nothing in My name.
Ask and you will receive, so that your joy
may be complete. (John 15:14-16; 16:
23-24 HCSB.)*

It is always a battle, whereby the enemy is trying
to use this wilderness opportunity to defeat you. So,
we need weapons in this warfare, in the world, and in
our lives. Good news: God has provided them for us.
I cannot over emphasize the great weapon of prayer.
This weapon will pull together and activate all the
weapons that He supplies for us to be overcomers in
every situation.

In the Ephesians 6 listing of the weapons that He
supplies, at the end of the list, "Praying always with
all prayer" (v. 18) is the foundation of them all. There
are different kinds, methods, and categories of prayer.
There is petition, supplication, and, as was instructed
here, intercession. Here is what is important when
you pray. You must do it with thanksgiving (see
Philippians 4:6); this is the assurance enveloped in
our prayer that we are the winners.

Referring to the previous Isaiah text, society's corruption contributed to what was going on at that time in Judah's history. The corruption was a diversion from what they knew they should have been doing in response. If God supplies what we need, His expectation is for us to use it. His expectation was for the women to intercede during this time.

The tendency is always to first stand and complain about the situation—clearly the wrong action. Prayer activates the promises of God and serves as a reminder to us of what He has promised, and God had promised to intervene.

Historically, physical walls were built for protection of a city's inhabitants during wars, and that's what they depended upon. However, they had to know that as strong as their wall was, it would not make them secure. The Spirit of the Living God would be their Defender.

Zechariah 4:6 declares, '"Not by might nor by power, but by My Spirit,' Says the Lord of hosts." Pray for God to intervene in the situation.

We cannot forget about *Faith.* We hear that word so often that it can become just a byword or a buzz word. Faith says, "I believe the God who has promised me in His word without any 'ifs, ands, or buts.'"

Faith is simply what Gods word says and we say Amen!

I believe God, though my wilderness looks terrible at this time. "Faith is...the evidence of things not seen" (Hebrews 11:1).

Importance of Worship in your wilderness – another great resource.

A worship center in the Wilderness.

When the children of Israel were in their wilderness, God told Moses, "Let them make Me a sanctuary, that I may dwell among them" (Exodus 25:8). These former slaves of Egypt had probably seen magnificent temples built for the gods of Egypt in the empire along the Nile. They had even helped construct some of them. Yet, as refugees in the wilderness, they had no central location for worshiping the God who had delivered them from bondage.

God knew the importance of them worshiping Him in their wilderness. I'm sure when the command was given to make a sanctuary (place of worship) they did not understand, especially when given the elaborate details of how they were to build it in the wilderness. God, who is a spirit and is everywhere, does not need a house to live in. His instruction was so He could dwell among them, not because He needed a place.

This wilderness was not their final place—neither is it yours.

Even though they were there a long time and they were destined to move through it, they still needed a place to worship. This sanctuary was for their benefit. God's eternal lesson to His people is we must always take time to worship no matter what the circumstance, the environment, or the situation.

"...by my Spirit, says the Lord of Hosts"
(Zechariah 4:6).

God promised never to leave or forsake us. (See Hebrews 13:5.) He has given His promise of the Spirit,

His presence, to be with us wherever we are. David learned this when he penned in Psalm 139:7-10, "Where can I [go to] flee from Your presence? ... If I make my bed in hell, behold, You are there. If I take the wings of the morning... Even there Your hand shall lead me." He is *there*, and how beautifully He manifests His presence through worship.

There are times in your wilderness that will be very dark. I call that time *a midnight hour* because, physically, that is the darkest hour just before dawn breaks. One of the greatest examples of worship to me is Paul and Silas as they worshiped in the midnight hour, as recorded in the book of Acts. (See Chapter 16.)

Let's visit them there, setting a scene from over two thousand years ago. We see it is just as relevant today, as we learn a lesson from them. They were thrown into a Roman prison, which was nothing less than a dungeon—no bathroom facilities, no lights, bound in chains that prevented any movement, and locks on every door. What did they do? prayed and worshiped. Something completely contrary to the human spirit.

They sang hymns (not about the human condition: "Get me out of here! You promised.") The hymns were worship songs: "Enter[ing] into His gates with thanksgiving, And into His courts with praise" (Psalm 100:4). Wherever you find yourself, you can enter His presence and build your own personal worship center. He inhabits the praises of His people. (See Psa. 22:3.) That is what God did. As we say: *He showed up.*

Oh yes, God showed up! Though He is always there, He now manifested Himself, by sending an earthquake that shook the place, and the doors were opened. Not just for Paul and Silas but every door that was in the prison was opened. You see, how you go through your wilderness may be deliverance for someone else. He still breaks yokes and looses us from bondage and from chains that bind us, no matter how strong they are.

Here is a great lesson while in your wilderness. God does things "exceedingly abundantly above all that we [can] ask or think" Ephesians 3:20). Not only did Paul and Silas receive what they needed, but also the surrounding prisoners heard their praise and worship. What a witness, as the other prisoners in a hopeless state were encouraged in their darkest hour.

The Lord continued to manifest Himself through Paul and Silas' praise and worship, and the miracle of physical deliverance came. They were set free. All the shackles that bound them were broken, and all the doors were opened. Though released from the physical bondage, God had greater plans. Purpose was all in their being free.

There was the jailer physically free, because he was not chained or behind locked doors. It was his job to watch prisoners, but he was still in bondage. He did not know Jesus, "the way, the truth, and the life" (John 14:6). He did not know that you would know the truth (Jesus), and this truth will set you free in every way. (See John 8:32.)

Your wilderness experience can be someone else's deliverance.

When Paul could have walked out, he stayed. Paul stayed in that environment, thinking on the things of others more than himself. (See Philippians 2:4.) The wilderness makes you more sensitive and caring for others, if you allow it. Those around you might not be experiencing the *same* experience as you, but you can use your situation to help someone else, even in the midst of your wilderness. There is always someone in a worse situation than you. *No pity party allowed!*

When you know the freedom found in Jesus Christ, you know that the most important freedom was being made free from sin. Receiving salvation by the blood of Jesus, which gives you eternal life, you can know that whatever situation you're in, you're still free. The jailer, when he saw the miracle-working hand of God and hears what Paul tells him, responds with: "What must I do to be saved?" (Acts 16:30).

Paul preached Jesus, who brings true deliverance when you know Him as Savior. Paul stayed until the jailer received Christ, and his entire household responded also. Prayer, Praise and Worship opened the prison doors; God manifested His presence; and an entire household was saved.

Your wilderness is a God-opportunity for praise, and a door that opens extends to others. God's got greater plans than you could ever imagine. Praise your God, worship, spend time with your Lord in your wilderness, and watch Him move and work. "Call [on] me, and I will answer you, and show you great and mighty things" (Jeremiah 33:3).

The importance of the presence of God and the anointing of God.

God's presence is His glory and His person. His anointing is His power, the manifestation, and the result of His presence. The promise in Acts 1:8 (NIV) "You will receive power when the Holy Spirit comes on you." Remember, when the Holy Spirit comes upon us, we are in the undeniable presence of God, accompanied by the power of His presence. The power brings the anointing to do the task—what God has for you to do while in the wilderness.

So, we must Access *The* Anointing.

How do I access the anointing?

The Greek word for anoint is *chrism* and means "to smear with His power." This is not just topical. This anointing will not only be *upon* us but *within* us, as oil rubbed *into* and then absorbed by the skin. The crushing of the olive produces oil that when emitted is what is needed for the task. Anointing will be the manifestation and the result of His presence. When the anointing hits a person, there is a divine charge and change! You will see things far beyond human achievement and accomplishment. Daniel said, "The people that do know their God shall be strong and do exploits" (Daniel 11:32 KJV).

The anointing brings change.

The anointing is the power of God upon and within people to fulfill spiritual assignments, break oppression, and catapult people into destiny. The greatest change will be in you, not in your environment, your wilderness.

Now you will see that part of your journey in the wilderness experience is God preparing you *for* and *to do* greater things. What the Spirit is doing *to* you, *in* you, and *for* you is what is happening here. God never calls someone to do something without providing an anointing! The anointing is always connected to **purpose.**

CHAPTER 4

MY WILDERNESS PURPOSE SETS ME APART

¹*To everything there is a season, A time for every purpose under heaven:*
² *A time to be born, And a time to die; A time to plant, And a time to pluck what is planted;* ³ *A time to kill, And a time to heal; A time to break down,*
And a time to build up;
⁴ *A time to weep, And a time to laugh; A time to mourn, And a time to dance;*
⁵ *A time to cast away stones, And a time to gather stones; A time to embrace,*
And a time to refrain from embracing;
⁶ *A time to gain, And a time to lose; A time to keep, And a time to throw away;*

*⁷ A time to tear, And a time to sew; A time
to keep silence, And a time to speak;
⁸ A time to love, And a time to hate; A
time of war, And a time of peace.
¹¹ He has made everything beautiful
in its time.*

(Ecclesiastic 3:1-8, 11 NKJV)

Life is a bit like a routine. You get up, go to the same job, pay the same bills every month, wondering if there's more to life than the *same old, same old*. You experience the defined seasons that Solomon listed in Ecclesiastes—a time for...

However, know that you were made with a purpose. You have a unique, customized calling on your life. God didn't make you because He was bored one day and wanted something to do. Every man and every woman were created for purpose, and He instilled in each one a purpose. You are the focus of all He has created. Although man was created first, if you are a woman, please know that you are not an afterthought once man was created.

We are made to glorify God. The expansion of His kingdom is a responsibility rooted in serving Him. This is the reason God made us. Even when man fell (and we will also in this journey), He will do for us just as He did for Adam and Eve, the first man and woman. He didn't leave them, nor will He leave us in that state. In the beginning, He promised to send a Savior, the purpose of which was to save us. This purpose was just the beginning. And for every season of your life, including this wilderness, God has a purpose and a time for its fulfillment.

Purpose is developed in seasons.

In the wilderness that the Israelites went through (40 years of seasons) the priests whom God had called apart and separated for purpose had to operate according to their calling as instructed by God. We, too, are called priests, set apart for the use of the Lord, and not just a priest, but also a "royal priest-hood" (1Peter 2:9). That's who we are and positioned as such.

Royalty has a higher standard and expectation but greater privileges. It's the king who makes the decisions for the citizens' lives. Sometimes our King, who is King of kings, decides to call us apart physically and emotionally from everything (wilderness). He is separating us for the purpose to anoint and to refocus us to who we are and what He wants us to do. Sometimes, one of the reasons is to make a *new* assignment/appointment.

Fighting against purpose.

We can get comfortable so easily where we are in the positions we have been operating in for a long time. We will fight like a junkyard dog over his territory to stay there and will not move. Our season may be up, and the anointing has left for it, and grace has been lifted. He has a new assignment for us. But we just don't want to leave that wonderful comfort zone that we fit in so beautifully and have for such a long time. And that comfort zone can be coupled with a fear of change. You don't have to fear because *Purpose is wrapped up with promises*. Going forward, taking the step of faith, each step will be surrounded with a promise. I now walk in the promises of God, who promises to complete those things concerning me.

Responding when I find myself in a wilderness.

What I should **not** do.

It's much easier to complain about your wilderness, prolonging the time. But it's better *to trust the God*—those four words—that allowed it so that His glory can be revealed through you, His servant.

Remember Joseph? He was really set apart for purpose. He was unjustly treated by his brothers, thrown into a pit, sold into slavery, and lied on by his employer's wife, resulting in his being thrown into prison. This was a total crushing of his character, influence, and birthright.

He was told through dreams and visions that he would be elevated to a position whereby even his brothers would bow down to him. Going through his wilderness, Joseph, never complained about the injustice. He simply served and did righteous acts that pleased God. He used each wilderness as an opportunity to help someone else. In doing so, he went from his varied wilderness experiences—from the pit to the palace. (See Genesis 37, 39-47.)

Hold on to your dream. It's time to reread your journal of promises to remind yourself what God has said to you in the light. Never doubt in the darkness (your wilderness) what God has spoken to you in the light.

Never allow the darkness of the wilderness to stop you from serving.

He will afford you opportunity to still be that servant that He has called. There are acts that the Holy Spirit can enable you to do while you are going through your wilderness. Listen to what He is saying; increase your time with Him when you find yourself there or as you *enter into that place.*

Are you entering into a wilderness?

How do I know? It's when things are getting worse and not better. You are praying, but it's not getting any better. You prayed—it stayed. You fast—it lasts. Your time and situation seem to be barren and not productive. Remember: "The steps of a good man are ordered by the Lord" (Psalm 37:23) even when you find yourself in a place that you absolutely do not want to be in. Rest in Him as He orders your steps at this time. Have a mind-set, not on yourself, but on the question: "How does He want to use me during my purpose/destiny at this time to bring glory to His name?"

Whatever action we take, the Spirit alone can multiply our efforts abundantly and beyond our expectations. (See Ephesians 3:20.) Each day, ask: "What can I do to be a help to someone else?" Look on the things of others more than on your own interests. (See Philippians 2:4.) There is focus again, but not on the environment, the circumstances, and the place, but on doing for someone else. There is always someone less fortunate than you.

> *As we take stands, act with righteousness, doing things for others even in our wilderness and the times of our wilderness we give the Spirit an opportunity to work, bless us and those that we help. (The Modern Life Study Bible)*

I wake up in the morning and find myself positioned in a place that I definitely don't want to be in. But my renewed mind (changed focus) says, "Who can I help today? Who in my sphere of influence can I let my light shine on in their darkness? Who in my haste and busyness have I passed by, not taking the time I should have to help? Jesus stopped on many occasions just for one person that was crying out for help, for people that were shunned by society at that time as hopeless. Just one word, one act of kindness from Him changed their lives entirely.

Seek the Lord for the purpose He has called you for. Allow Him to confirm it and enlarge it as you move forward into the direction of your destiny. This wilderness is just a tool to charge you, build you, and perfect those things concerning you.

CHAPTER 5

THAT WONDERFUL GRACE — IN THE WILDERNESS

When Mercy cried... Grace answered.

The Power of God's Grace
Romans 5:1-5

Therefore, having been justified by faith, we have peace with God through our Lord Jesus Christ, ² through whom also we have access by faith into this grace in which we stand, and rejoice in hope of the glory of God. ³ And not only that, but we also glory in tribulations, knowing that tribulation produces perseverance; ⁴ and perseverance, character; and character, hope. ⁵ Now hope does not disappoint,

*because the love of God has been poured
out in our hearts by the Holy Spirit who
was given to us.*

Grace is one of God's most amazing gifts. The sustaining power of God is packaged in His grace. It provides us with everything we need to live in perfect freedom. He specializes in replacing guilt with grace, granting pardon for our sins, and healing for our hearts. We have the companionship of God's indwelling Holy Spirit and access to freely cultivate our relationship with Him. It's that *Amazing grace.*

We work, worship, and enjoy life surrounded by His unconditional love. His grace upholds us, fills us, and sustains us in the good times—but most importantly— in the bad times of our wilderness experiences. When we cry out to Him in our wilderness, grace answers with all its components. What a great shot in the arm, the encouragement it is that lifts up my head when disappointments loom heavily upon me.

Let's hear the Apostle Paul's personal testimony he records to the church at Corinth on the Lord's **great grace:**

2 Corinthians 12:7-10

> [7] *And lest I should be exalted above mea-*
> *sure by the abundance of the revelations,*
> *a thorn in the flesh was given to me, a*
> *messenger of Satan to buffet me, lest I*
> *be exalted above measure.* [8] *Concerning*
> *this thing...*

Oh my! Paul, you saw that there was a **purpose** for your wilderness experience. *God never does things haphazardly; He always has a purpose, and it's always for our good.*

Paul immediately activates his privilege of prayer even in the midst of this disappointing first statement of what the purpose was for *his thorn*. He had a petition, causing him to spend time with his Lord. As he repeatedly made this request, God answers.

Listen to Paul's further words:

> *I pleaded with the Lord three times that*
> *it [the thorn] might depart from me.* [9]
> *And He said to me, "My grace is sufficient*

for you, for My strength is made perfect in weakness." Therefore most gladly I will rather boast in my infirmities, that the power of Christ may rest upon me. 10 Therefore I take pleasure in infirmities, in reproaches, in needs, in persecutions, in distresses, for Christ's sake. For when I am weak, then I am strong.

Are you kidding, Paul? You can take pleasure in your infirmities, in reproaches, every need, and persecutions? Though there was a thorn, you can forget about the thorn because His grace is greater.

As my friend, Lydia, says: "When you grow roses, in each bush, there are thorns; and it is inevitable that once in a while, a thorn will prick your finger. But the beauty of the roses overshadows the thorns that are in there. Why would you chance missing the beautiful fragrant roses because of a small thorn?"

Yes, dear reader, because of Grace...

The Power of Grace is more than enough, measured against what you are going through. God's grace enables us to go from strength to strength through all the trials. It settles me into His perfect will for my life, delivering that peace that says, "Not My will, but Yours be done" (Luke 22:42). "You know what's best for me and what it will take for me to be all that You want me to be and desire of my life."

It is sufficient for me. He takes that weakest point in my life in or resulting from my wilderness experience and imperfect strength, I can in turn rest because Christ's rest is upon me. It's taking His yoke upon us, as Matthew says, "For [His] yoke is easy and [His] burden is light" (Matthew 11:30). I will experience the truth of His promise, His strength being made perfect in my weakness.

That wonderful privilege of praying in my wilderness, praying into the will of God.

Wait is such an important part of this ... that I don't like. Again, prayer is an important part of waiting on the Lord. We can go to the Lord at any time and in our own words. He hears us wherever and whatever the circumstance, and when we struggle to find the words, He provides us with Scripture that we can use to pray.

He sees us as what we can be and what He wants us to be. The Lord responds to us, not as strangers or enemies, but as His dearly loved children. (See Romans 8:15; Ephesians 5:1.) Does He hear our prayers? His ears are open to the cry of the righteous. (See Psalms 34:15.) And He will speak to us, communicate with us, and act on our behalf, doing *through* us far greater than what we could ever do. That is why we can "wait on the Lord [and] be of good courage" (Psalms 27:14) as we wait.

It is through this Grace that He gives in the Wilderness that God amply supplies us with so many other benefits.

The knowledge that we live under the covering of God's grace also lets us know even more of these benefits. He is never limited; in fact, He pours out grace to us.

There is security in our *position* in Christ. No one can snatch us out of His hand. (See John 10:28.) Remember the lame man's position was physical, lying in a place without hope except some man come and rescue him. Our position in Christ is much more powerful. We don't have to wait or depend on *a* man, but *the* Man, Christ Jesus, Emmanuel, God with us, who is always there. The wilderness we are going through—it cannot, will not separate us from His love. (See Romans 8:38-39.) Indeed, the position is that we are held in His hand. Now, what is closer than that?

CHAPTER 6

LESSONS FROM THE POTTER'S HOUSE

"The word which came to Jeremiah from the Lord, saying: 'Arise and go down to the potter's house, and there I will cause you to hear my [voice]'" (Jeremiah 18:1-2).

T he Lord will lead us, cause us, and instruct us to go places where we can hear and learn from Him. Jeremiah learns this lesson when God told him to go down to the potter's house. He saw a potter shaping a vessel on the wheel with his hands. When there was a flaw while he was making this vessel—and life will do that—he simply made it again. But the key was, though flawed, it was still in the potter's hand.

The wilderness experience is a molding and making experience for us. God, who created us, wants us to be the best that we can be, and He knows what it takes. We would often settle for less, but God wants the best out of us—removing the flaws (those things that are taking away from us being whole, complete, and mature).

God's people, while going through the vast persecution from their enemy, felt He was forgetting them, and thereby they were experiencing this terrible loneliness. God gave them such a wonderful example when He said, "Can a [mother] forget her nursing child, And not have compassion on the son of her womb?" (Isaiah 49:15).

There is nothing closer than a mother nursing her child. Any mother that nurses knows it is a biological impossibility to forget that child. The milk will emerge at the exact feeding time of that baby. You have no choice but to stop and nurse, and there can be no delay. The need is inscribed in the mother's very body, corresponding with the child's need. Wherever she may be, the mother has to go and get the baby and meet that need. In fact, there are some times when the baby's cry will activate the milk. How awesome is that! It's so true of God's perfect order for us.

When His children cry, when they have a need wherever they are, it activates our Father's heart to meet that need. *Hallelujah!* He told the prophet, *they* (the mother) *could* forget before He *would*.

God used this as a parable, but He tells them He is so much greater. Continued in verse 16, He proclaims through Isaiah, "See, I have inscribed you on the palms of My hands; Your walls are continually before Me." He said He had engraved them (are those tattoos?) in the palms of His hands. What a great position! Your hands are always with you. Because they are attached and because you use them often, their presence cannot be forgotten, as they are joined to you and are always before you. Isn't that great? Every time the Lord moves His hands, He sees you. He says that you are ever before Him; that hand also covers you and moves on your behalf. That hand is your *wall* (protection).

Back to the potter: After the vessel has been formed and the flaws removed, it must go into the kiln, where the fire seals it. It does not stay in there too long but for just enough time to complete the work. It's similar to gold that has to be placed in the fire to burn off all of the dross to make it pure. Job said, during his wilderness experience, "When He has tested me, I shall come forth as [pure] gold" (Job 23:10).

We would settle for just having the gold, a wonderful vessel, but God will not allow us to settle for anything less. We are going to *look good*, as the gold does, but, as well, *be good* like pure gold, which is profitable to all we encounter and have endurance. He wants us to be not just a conversation piece that sits on a mantle for display but also active for use. We are treasures "in earthen vessels," so that the power of God can shine through us. (See 2 Corinthians 4:7.)

Most of us know about Job's wilderness experiences. If not, take time to read about them as he details them in the book named for him. He came out of his wilderness better than he went into it. He received double for all of his trouble. That's the beauty of serving our Lord: It all works together for our good, and we will come out of that wilderness *better* than we went into it (His purpose). "All things work together for good...according to *His purpose*" (Rom. 8:28 emphasis mine).

We have a Covenant of Grace with Him.

Living under God's covenant of Grace also gives us:

- **Boldness** to live for Christ. After we have been through the wilderness experience, experiencing the presence of the Holy Spirit and His grace, nothing anyone does or says can shake our confidence in who the Lord is or who we are in Him. I recall the refrain in an old familiar gospel hymn by Margaret P. Douroux that we used to sing in church and was based on what King David said in Psalm124, "If it had not been for the Lord on my side, tell me where would I be, where would I be?"

- The **Peace** that passes all understanding. (See Philippians 4:7.) When the false peace that the world promises quickly dissipates, especially in the time we are now living in, we can have this peace because we can fully trust in His sovereignty. It is not according to the dictates of the world's agreements, treaties, or the present administrations that are heading countries' peace stipulations. The Lord is carrying out His perfect will. And we can be sure that nothing is able to thwart His plans when we cooperate with Him. Our hope is in Him, the Prince of Peace.

What about the future...my future?

This hope extends much further than the present situation. It also extends into the future. This abundant life is just the beginning: the opening of doors that no man can shut; living the life that He has promised you and receiving the promises He has afforded you; being in health and prospering as your soul prospers. What a great future is promised us. I am not here to stay in this situation; God has greater plans for me. This wilderness is preparing me for things I cannot see or even fathom.

The best of our future?

One day we'll see Jesus face to face, be perfected as the individuals He created us to be, and live with Him in our true home forever. True home? yes, don't forget that "our citizenship is in heaven" (Philippians 3:20). We are just strangers passing through to a promised land that has been prepared for us.

The Lord is committed to transforming each of us according to His special plan for our lives.

Even when the wilderness is a correction, His correction is an expression of His loving favor. A good father chastises his child when he sees him going in a direction that is harmful and will not be conducive to his growth, to turn him in the right direction that is good and not destructive. He does this because He loves him and wants the very best for his child. So much more does our heavenly Father, who goes a step further when we falter or fail. We can rest assured that His amazing grace surrounds us and always offers us redemption. That's who He is.

CHAPTER 7

THE *WHO* VERSUS THE *WHAT*

*Our Focus—**Who** He is; Not **what's** happening to us?*

It is so easy to focus on ourselves during the trials in our life, understandably so because it is **what is happening to *me*?** But it's our reaction to the trial that is important. I can verbally speak positively about it, even quoting a biblical promise that applies to it. However, speaking the promise but looking at the trial and pronouncing the actuality produces no expectation. I call it ***backward Christianity***.

You can ***not*** have backward Christianity expecting results:

"I know God is able to supply all my needs (see Philippians 4:19), *but* my finances are in the toilet!"

"I know He is peace and will give joy, but I'm so stressed out I don't know what to do!"

That is reaching **back** to the problem that now becomes greater than the Problem Solver.

Onward Christian Soldiers; not *backward* Christian Soldiers! You can *not* proclaim His Word (the promises) and then look back at the situation and declare something else *negatively*.

It's Who God Is.

He is Jehovah Jireh, my Provider, and more than enough! For He is also El-Shaddai. My finances may be in the toilet, but my God promised to supply all of my need according to HIS riches in Glory, not mine. (See Philippians 4:19, emphasis mine.) I expect Him to be all that He has promised to be in my life. And He *will*, for He cannot lie. In fact, Hebrews 6:18 says, "It is impossible for God to lie."

He is Jehovah Roe. "The Lord is my Shepherd [and] I shall not want" (Psalm 23:1).

He is Jehovah Raphe, *The Lord that heals.* (See Exodus 15:26.) "And by his stripes, [I am] healed" (Isaiah 53:5). This is a promise that was made before, initiated at His passion, executed at Calvary, and confirmed the third day when He arose from the grave as an overcomer. All power is in His hand. (See Matthew 28:18.)

I can now look at things the way they *are* and declare them the way they will be. I learned this when I went through a healing process of a wound on my leg. When that wound had been there for many months and was not getting any better, the Lord reminded me, "It takes God to heal a wound" and that He was my healer. This worship song came to me, as I changed my bandage each day and the wound would look worse than before: "He's healing me and I'm going to worship." So, as I changed the bandage, I sang that song, not seeing it as it *was* but seeing it as God declared it to be. I was just going to worship Him. Today, I proclaim victory, as the wound is totally healed!

He is Jehovah Elohim...*Lord God*. "The Lord, He is God" (Psa. 100:3), and He is over everything. He is in control no matter what the situation looks like and things appear *out of control. He is still in control.* He is Lord. "Every knee will bow...and every tongue should confess that Jesus Christ is Lord" (Philippians 2:10-11 HCSB). As my husband used to say, "All means just that—ALL! If He cannot be Lord *of all*, He will not be Lord *at all.*" It is the same with your personal life. If He cannot be Lord *of all*, He will not be Lord *at all.*

He is Love personified.

We long for such unconditional love. Yet the wounds, disappointments, and mistakes we experience can make us feel anything but loved. But God opens His arms—the arms of a perfect Father—and invites us into them to experience and **rest** in his love as we wait on His perfect timing for our lives. We know what the wilderness is and what we experience is real. But it is all negative when we leave the author and finisher of our faith out of it.

Rest is the positive position in your wilderness.

The wilderness can be a resting place, a holding pattern: a place God holds you until His perfect time for you to move.

Rest seems to be a word that is foreign to us these days in our busy lives. We sleep, but we don't rest. The testimony of so many is "I'm exhausted," and they don't see the ramifications that stem from the reasons for their exhaustion.

We don't take time to *smell the roses*. Remember that phrase? We dig, we plant, we weed, we prune but never stop to enjoy the fruit of our labor. It's on to the next planting, weeding, pruning, etc.

We forge ahead on our own paths, believing this is what we do. Even vacations are a time of spent energy that many times we need a vacation to recover *from* our vacations! Our to-do list— we can't do without them; how else will we be organized? — trumps our lives. We have gone to the extremes of serving, working where we have forgotten how to care for ourselves ...*red flag*!

God, our Creator, is so smart (knowing His creation) that He saw this from the very beginning. His creation did not have the sense to stop and just rest— the reason for the Sabbath. God had to instruct them to rest. For the Sabbath's 24 hours, they had to rest, which meant ceasing from all their labors. When He said rest, it was to do absolutely nothing. There was no cooking, no working, not even any traveling on the Sabbath. After the Jews observed the Sabbath, they had celebrations. See the balance? So very simple, yet so very hard for us to do.

Sometimes it's to be in complete silence, being still; and other times, it's to go and enjoy, play, spend time with others, and break the work barrier to change your focus. God said, "Be still, and know that I am God" (Psalms 46:10). We need to be still to hear from Him and watch the course of change He sometimes wants to make in our lives. *Be still* to hear the still small voice that Elijah almost missed when he looked for God in the thunder, the fire, the wind, the storm, and the hurricane. (See 1 Kings 19:11-13.) Even though God had showed up many times in those ways previously, it was the still small voice after the fire that spoke to him.

Exhaustion brings anxiety. Impatiently, we will rush into things without considering **timing**— what the Lord is saying NOW to us. Our plans, though well-thought-out and examined in detail for success, just may not be His plans for us.

When we are overly anxious for something, we don't consider time. Perhaps it's not time for me to receive what has been promised. We need to learn how to rest and listen and when it is time, His time, it will come to pass. Let's see how Caleb said it. After embracing God's 45-year promise: "He spoke loudly with confidence, I have served the Lord wholeheartedly, now He has kept me alive for this time. So here I am today, still as strong, now give me this hill country that the Lord promised me that day.... (Joshua14:10).

Elijah, the great prophet, was exhausted after that great feat and success on Mount Carmel. The drought that God used him to predict finally ended after over three years. (See 1 Kings 17-18.)

Can you imagine? Picture this: The land is dry after 3 ½ years of no rain and resulting famine. The whole land of Israel is a wilderness. Nothing but dry brown dirt, constant dehydration of the people, and crops failing consistently... Yet in this wilderness, Elijah speaks and tells King Ahab that they should prepare themselves because it is getting ready to rain.

God used Elijah in this wilderness to speak using the authority given to him so that everyone would benefit. It is recorded in I Kings 18:46 that when the rain finally started and came pouring down, Elijah actually outran Ahab's chariot. Talk about running sprints! He was champion.

But sadly, exhaustion was the word for him after this feat. When we are exhausted, we open ourselves up to the enemy's voice that can become louder than God's. Immediately after this, he got this news...

He was the top item on Queen Jezebel's to-do list. And that was to kill him. He ran again; this time out of fear. At a very vulnerable point in his life, he feared one person—a woman. Fear and exhaustion, a very bad combination, moved into depression.

Depression breeds loneliness, which moved into self-pity with the results of Elijah praying, "It is enough! Now, Lord, [just] take my life" . That was certainly not a prayer of hope, faith or confidence. (1 Kings 19:4). Elijah moved into the exile of a cave, a cave *after* standing on a mountain challenging 400 prophets of Baal, winning with the Lord God who answered his request by fire and declaring rain on the wilderness of Israel after 3 ½ years.

No matter how high your mountain-top experience or the powerful experiences of moments that were God moments in your life, you can experience wilderness of your soul, body, and strength.

God had to call him out of the cave first before He could speak to him and give him directions. And the directions came in a ***still small voice***

Running for my life.

What does the Lord have to say to you if you are on this treadmill of running and running but not seeming to get anywhere at this time? All it is producing is exhaustion.

It's the same word He gave to His people hundreds of years ago, who had the same problem. The account is given in Isaiah 30:15-18 (NIV) where God's people thought they were moving ahead at a fast pace, but they were on a treadmill because their movement was out of His will. What were they doing? They had moved into getting nowhere by looking to other sources for their advancement and protection and not to Jehovah God. Ours is a treadmill; theirs was labeled as horses. When you step out of the will of God, no matter how hard you try, it can have dangerous consequences. How can they be saved from their misdirections? It was their ***Plan B***, if you will, and God speaks to them saying the following:

> [15] *In repentance and rest is your salvation,*
>
> *in quietness and trust is your strength,*
>
> *but you would have none of it.*
>
> [16] *You said, 'No, we will flee on horses.'*
>
> *Therefore you will flee!*
>
> *You said, 'We will ride off on swift horses.'*
>
> *Therefore your pursuers will be swift!*
>
> [17] *A thousand will flee*
>
> *at the threat of one;*
>
> *at the threat of five*
>
> *you will all flee away,*
>
> *till you are left*
>
> *like a flagstaff on a mountaintop,*
>
> *like a banner on a hill. (vv. 15-17)*

There is no *Plan B* with God.

God was saying, "Stop what you are doing, trust Me, and rest in Me." The word used is *repent* from what you are doing. The word *repentance* really means changing directions, to turn from. Running, no matter how fast you are, is not getting you anywhere but moving you in the wrong direction. Coupled with that is depending on sources that you do not have to depend on. But God does not leave them in this environment of hopelessness because...

Hear the word of *grace* again:

> Yet the Lord longs to be gracious to you;
> therefore he will rise up to show you compassion.
> For the Lord is a God of justice.
> Blessed are all who wait for him! (v. 18)
> Stop running ahead, and wait on Him for His directions.

God patiently directs us as we trust Him and listen for His voice.

One expression of God's graciousness is His promise to guide us by His Spirit. That happens as we take the time to talk to Him about our desires and ask in prayer what He has for us. Be thankful that God patiently directs us, day-by-day, step-by-step, as we trust Him and listen for His voice each step of the way.

As my nephew, CJ Blair, said that he found out in his life, "God does *everything in steps*; therefore, no steps are wasted, missed, or backward. All steps work for your good. You must endure the fight to determine if you truly believe everything God said. Trust the process."

Don't try to get out of your wilderness—*your way.* If you do, God, as He did during the time of His people's restlessness in the Isaiah scriptural example above, is asking you to *return and rest.* In fact, their deliverance was contingent on their rest. But sad to say, the people's response was "No," and instead, they speeded up, as we sometimes do on our own course, plans, and treadmills.

Resting is a place God alone can provide in my wilderness.

This is not a rest because of physical tiredness; however, that also could be a factor for my being in this wilderness. I have also an *emotional* tiredness that can be as tedious and taxing and also more damaging than a physical tiredness.

It can be:

- **A chronic sickness** that the medication is only relieving for a season, and the medication is becoming more of a detriment. Soon the doctor will prescribe another one to counteract the previous one. **Lord, how long?**
- **Marriage** that's on a roller coaster that when I think it's getting better, a situation happens that puts us back at ground zero, it seems. **Lord, how long?**
- **Children**...running a treadmill of troubles from one situation to another, never seeming to get anywhere, just exhausted and in the same place. **Lord, how long?**
- **Finances**...that dip more than rise above what I need. **Lord, how long?**
- **My profession**, advancements, school, degree...in this, my wilderness of waiting... **Lord**, how long?
- Will **The One** (spouse) that's destined for me to spend the rest of my life with ever come? Lonely...**Lord, how long?**

Others pass me, go home with theirs', celebrate anniversaries, children's birthdays... And then they have the audacity to say to me in their (what seems like superficial smugness), "Just pray, be encouraged, just wait on the Lord." As they depart with their spouse, I am not encouraged because they really don't understand.

> *I've learned and often tell my children,*
> *"Never leave God out of the equation*
> *no matter how it looks at the time."*
> *Herldleen Russell*

Look again at what God supplies in the wilderness. He creates a resting place for His children. It's not just a place to sit down and twiddle your thumbs waiting for the next move, but it's a rest in Him, knowing His timing is perfect. This rest is while I wait for it to "work together for [my] good" (Romans 8:28) for He has promised. I can wait, and He will teach me how to wait. Not just waiting, but waiting **well**.

It's a place of re-establishing communication. Not silence or loneliness.

It's a place where there is just you and God. God told His people that He called them into the wilderness whereby He could speak to them. Sometimes in the busyness of life, God can't get our attention. Have you willfully gone in a direction, though it might seem to be a good direction for you in this season of your life? It's a good direction moving towards your goal; however, it just may not be the route He wants you to take. Rest; see what He has to say about it. It's that simple. Stop and listen. Hear what He is saying. *Rushing* is not *Resting*.

Rest in His unconditional love.

"God is love" (1 John 4:8), and we rest in *who* He is. His love covers a multitude of sins. There is no condemnation in His love, even when we make mistakes. "His compassions fail not. They are new every morning; great is [His] faithfulness" (Lamentation 3:22-23). He knows me better than anyone else, even myself; yet, He still loves me and wants the best for me. I can rest in these truths.

Conditions cannot separate me from His ever-lasting, unconditional love. The apostle Paul even gave us a list of some of these things when he wrote to the church at Rome acknowledging the perils that he was going through:

> *What then shall we say to these things?*
> *If God is for us, who can be against us?*
> *He who did not spare His own Son, but*
> *delivered Him up for us all, how shall*
> *He not with Him also freely give us all*
> *things? (Romans 8:31-32)*

His Love demonstrated at a great cost.

> *Who [what] shall separate us from the*
> *love of Christ? Shall tribulation, or dis-*
> *tress, or persecution, or famine, or*
> *nakedness, or peril, or sword...Yet in*
> *all these things we are more than con-*
> *querors through Him who loved us. For I*
> *am persuaded that neither death nor life,*

nor angels nor principalities nor powers,
nor things present nor things to come,
nor height nor depth, nor any other cre-
ated thing, shall be able to separate us
from the love of God which is in Christ
Jesus our Lord. (vv. 35, 37-39)

In fact, He declares, "We are more than conquerors" in every situation because of His love. We
are not defeated. Not just conquering the situation
but *more than*, exceedingly abundantly above all that
we ask or think. I can rest in His love in my wilderness
experience because nothing, absolutely nothing, can
separate me from His love.

So come the questions, with all these truths
and promises.

"Why don't I rest? Why am I not applying these
promises to my life?" Simply because of unbelief,
God said "They entered not in[to my rest] because of
unbelief." Hebrews 4:6 (KJV). It's one thing to *know* a
fact, but it's another thing to *believe* what you know.

The Lord spoke to me, personally, when I was vacillating back and forth about a situation and said, "When are you going to start believing what you know?" How simple but powerful was that? *It's time to start believing what you know* because **knowing** is only half the battle. Many **know** what it takes, but not everybody will **do** what it takes.

A great thought from Dr. Charles Stanley on obedience and disobedience...

It started at the beginning of time. The Creator gave two commands to Adam and Eve—first, to fill the earth and rule over it, and second, not to eat from a certain tree in the Garden (Gen 1:28, 2:17). Because they chose to disobey, their relationship with God was broken, and they had to leave this wonderful garden, a paradise.

The first couple's rebellion not only impacted their own lives but also had far broader implications: all future generations have suffered. In Romans 5:12-19, the apostle Paul explained the reason. Through the trespass of one man, Adam, sin made its entrance into the world, and death resulted for all mankind.

Because Adam was head of the human race, his actions affected everyone born after him. His disobedience resulted in each of us having a bent away from the Lord and a desire for self-rule.

By contrast, Jesus made conformity to the Lord's will the priority of His life. He obeyed God in both word and deed (See John 8:28-29) having lived a perfect life—one entirely without sin—He qualified to be our Savior. Through the death of one man, Christ Jesus, payment was made for the transgressions of all mankind. God's acceptance of the Son's sacrifice brought us forgiveness and freedom from sin's power.

Adam and Eve knew what God had said, but did they believe what He said? The consequences of disobedience were detrimental. The ripple of disobedience will not only be seen in your life, but can rivet through your family and generations. God gave us a way of escape through Jesus Christ, our Lord. So we don't have to bow to the tactics of the enemy. We are not only free but have freedom from sin's power. All we have to do is believe what we know and act on it. We will discover the amazing God that shows up in our wilderness, giving us all of the benefits that He affords us when we **REST** and Trust Him.

So the question will always come and it repeats again as at the first of this book. *Will you trust me now? Will you choose to do it my way?*

CHAPTER 8

I WILL GROW AND MATURE IN MY WILDERNESS

"Lord, my heart is not proud; my eyes are not haughty. I don't concern myself with matters too great or too awesome for me to grasp. Instead, I have calmed and quieted myself, like a weaned child who no longer cries for its mother's milk" (Psalms131:1-2 NLT).

Remember the mother and nursing child that God reminds His people as an example of how He will never forget them? I believe the writer in Psalms 131 is now saying "I have learned that there is nothing so great that my God cannot handle." So now he has learned not to concern himself with matters too great or awesome. They belong to his God. Therefore, he calms and quiets himself like a weaned child who no longer cries for its mother's milk. He doesn't cry about every little thing, though he remains a teachable child. Sometimes a baby is not hungry, and when it cries, its cry is not to eat but to just nestle in his mother's arms. Like little children, we can learn to rest in the love of God. Romans 8:15 says we can call upon Him as *Abba Father,* a term of endearment, (i.e.) *Poppa, Daddy.* Imagine climbing up into His lap and just snuggling up into those great big arms, resting.

Maturing in our wilderness, we can let go of the battle in our mind over what we don't understand, trusting in the One who fights our battle. We are never to lean to our own understanding, but instead, through time with Him, acknowledge Him in all of our ways. We can return to a place of peace, finding the hope we need in His love; yet, become as calm and quiet as if we were children again in our parent's arms. This is total trust.

Total Trust is a must.

"Commit your way to the Lord; trust in Him, and he will act, making our righteousness shine like the dawn, your justice like the noonday" (Psalms 37:5-6 HCSB). Being silent before the Lord is, again, nestling in His arms, finding "the secret place...under the shadow of the almighty" (Psalms 91:1), "and wait[ing] expectantly for Him").

Maturing, yet remaining as a child...

> *"But grow in grace, and in the knowledge of our Lord and Savior Jesus Christ" (2 Peter 3:18 KJV).*

> *"Except ye... become as little children ..."*
> *(Matthew 18:3 KJV)*

We forget that our faith journey is one of consistently learning as little children, learning God's ways and coming to the knowledge of truth of who He is, and then, as a son patterns his life after his Dad, living out what he has learned from him. It doesn't take a lot of faith on our journey—just the "faith as a grain of mustard seed" (Matthew 17:20 KJV), believing our Father for the results. We need to activate the measure of faith He gives us and learn to keep our focus and dependence on Him.

If we lose focus, we can find ourselves missing out on all God has already given us, much like the older brother in Jesus' parable of the prodigal son, trying desperately to win his father's approval. (See Luke 15:25-32.) This son's place was a place of entitlement and anxiety—not a place of appreciation, gratitude, and trust. He had lost the child-like wonder and excitement of trusting his daddy, trusting his decisions and being refreshingly surprised daily as he cares for him and does what he knows is best for his child. What your Father has for you—it's for you— and no one can take it from you. It is written and declared in His last will and testament, sealed and this His perfect will for you, can never be challenged or broken.

This is the child that pleases His Father: one that grow[s]in grace, and in the knowledge of our Lord and Savior Jesus Christ. Growth does not mean you will not have problems or make mistakes. Growth pains are a reality. The child that first learns to walk will stumble and fall some times, but he does not lie there; he gets up and continues. Beside him is the loving parent that encourages him to get up and continue trying because the parent knows this is the only way the child's walk will be perfected. "Though he fall, he shall not be utterly cast down; For the Lord upholds him with His hand. (Psalms 37:24-25)

I have been young, and now am old; Yet I have not seen the righteous forsaken, Nor his descendants begging bread.

That child, as he grows, will experience problems in his life—some that are easily solved, some that are bigger than he or she ever anticipated in life. He soon learns that life happens to the best-laid plans. But as he grows and learns to lean on and trust his daddy, he will come to know that his daddy will always be there. This Daddy is not a dead beat or an absentee landlord. He is his present help in the time of every trouble. (See Psalms. 46:1.)

Our perfect Father's presence is there in every situation; but more than that (and not like our earthly father who is limited no matter how wonderful he is), our heavenly Father delivers out of every situation. "The Lord's hand is not shortened, That it cannot save; Nor His ear heavy, That it cannot hear" (Isaiah 59:1). "Many are the afflictions of the righteous, But the Lord delivers him out of them all" (Psalms. 34:19).

Every problem is for purpose, for building character, and making us strong. None comes to destroy us because Father allows it, and the situation can go no further than what He allows. This wilderness will not envelop us or consume us. It is ordered to work together for our good. We need it to continue this journey that He has blueprinted for our lives. Every trial we experience works together for our good. Each trial and those things which concern us are designed just for us to mature and perfect us so that we can be people of purpose and destiny to glorify our Father. This is why we can praise through our growth experiences. In everything, I can give thanks because it is the will of God for those who belong to Christ Jesus. For those that belong to Christ Jesus—I am not alone. There is "a huge crowd of witnesses" that Hebrews 12:1 speaks of that went before me who were challenged and experienced wildernesses in their lives. They are now the example for me as I read about them *in* and coming *out* of their wilderness experiences victoriously, seeing God's plan for their lives.

CHAPTER 9

THE CORRIDORS OF FAITH

Some of the greatest heroes of faith went through a wilderness.

The people, the places and the experiences.

Moses began his wilderness experience on the backside of a mountain. He neither anticipated nor desired an encounter with the Lord. He had killed an Egyptian man and had to flee from Egypt. He was living a quiet shepherd's life in Median with his wife and family. But God had heard His people's cries for help and had chosen Moses as the man who would deliver them from slavery. (**You** just might be an answer to someone's prayer!)

So, God initiated this meeting on the backside of that mountain by showing up in a burning bush that was not being consumed. It was common for a bush to catch on fire in the dry desert from the heat combustion, but this one caught Moses' attention because it was not being consumed. God knows how to get our attention so that He can speak to us.

Emanating from that burning bush came these words: "Draw not nigh hither: put off thy shoes from off thy feet, for the place whereon thou standest is holy ground" (Exodus 3:5 KJV). That wilderness place became holy ground whereby Moses was instructed to take off his shoes, stand, and be confronted by God, Himself. *Take off your shoes* was part of God's first directive; for Moses' directions were getting ready to change and his destiny executed from that place.

The wilderness is where we are afforded the opportunity to take off things that will hinder our destiny.

In obedience, Moses took off his shoes as he met with His God. As it always does, meeting God launched him on an incredible journey. God's choice of the place is His for our meeting with Him.

What did Moses receive in his wilderness experience? not only new directions, but even more so, the silencing of all his fears of the great task in front of him by God's promise of His presence. God's presence, Moses would find, was more than enough to complete what God had given him to do when he left the wilderness. His presence was in the wilderness and would always be with Him as he walked in obedience. Moses would return to that place, better known as Mount Sinai, but the next time he stood there, he would be a transformed man.

John the Baptist was called out of a physical wilderness from eating locusts and wild honey, which had been a time of preparation for his extraordinary responsibility to preach the gospel of repentance and be the forerunner of Jesus Christ. His wilderness experience, unique as it was, strengthened him to continue his ministry. He was a very humble man. Though he was center stage during this time, he never tried to take the credit for how God was using him so profoundly. He stayed in the lane that God had ordained for his life. He recognized his position, not trying to take anyone else's or be anyone else.

Though he had great responsibilities for which he was recognized and had disciples that followed him, he never took the glory because he recognized that it belonged to Jesus. John said, "He (Jesus) must increase, but I must decrease" (John 3:30). Jesus said of him (John) that out of all the prophets in history, there was none greater than John the Baptist. (See Luke 7:28.) How committed was John to obedience, to righteousness? Humble, but courageous. Knowing his purpose, he challenged even the throne upon which the king sat. (See Luke 3:19.) It cost him his life on earth, but he received eternal life. "Well done, good and faithful servant" (Matthew 25:23).

John the Baptist's purpose was greater than the price paid.

What about you? Do you know your purpose? Are you willing to pay the price for your purpose? Are you willing to do the following? To go through a wilderness to fine-tune your character, strengthen you, initiate, and confirm your purpose? To **not** try to duplicate someone else's purpose or be like anyone else but you—that amazing person that God made—and to glorify Him? Oh, just to hear Him (and no one else) say, "Well done, good and faithful servant; you have been faithful over a few things, I will make you ruler over many things. Enter into the joy of your lord" (Matthew 25:23).

Jesus experienced His wilderness where Satan, himself, showed up in his attempt to turn Jesus' destiny into a direction totally against His Father's will for His life with the temptations that are common to man: "the lust of the flesh, the lust of the eyes, and the pride of life" (1 John 2:16). He became the example to us that we can overcome any temptation that is common to man by the Word of God and see God provide, as promised, a way of escape. We can be more than conquerors because of our wilderness. Jesus came out of that wilderness, not weakened, but in the power of the Holy Ghost. (See Luke 4:14.)

Jesus experienced His Gethsemane, the garden where He fell on His face and asked God if it was at all possible to take this cup (the dreaded crucifixion) from Him, if there was any other way God could accomplish His purpose in Him. But as He prayed, He moved into a place called *the perfect will* of His Father, a rest. He experienced the grace that only comes from the Father, the ministry of angels, and the peace that passes all understanding.

God empathizes with us in our suffering and wilderness place as He is touched with the feeling of our infirmities.

Did you consider that God, the Father, suffered in the garden as well? This was not a one-sided affair. The Father and the Son shared intimate fellowship from all eternity. God was able to empathize because this suffering was a shared experience. And if God empathized with Christ, if He made a way for Christ, won't He make a way for us too? **Hallelujah!** So, Jesus was able to pray through and say, "Not My will, but Yours, be done" (Luke 22:42). The Apostle, Paul, picks it up in Hebrews 12:2 showing us the experience, the purpose, and the destiny: "Who for the joy that was set before Him endured the cross, despising the shame, and has sat down at the right hand of the throne of God."

You can place your name here among the great: _____. Write your wilderness experience, now knowing the grace He gives and the promises that accompany it.

CHAPTER 10

WHEN YOU *THINK* YOUR WILDERNESS IS THE END OF IT ALL ...YOUR FINAL DESTINATION

The gospel of Mark records two distinct and different cases that overlap in one chapter. (See Mark 5:22-43.) There was a man named Jairus, a leader in his community, who had a daughter that was very ill. We don't know how long she had had this illness, but now she was dying as a result. He heard that Jesus, who was miraculously healing people—the blind's sight restored, the lame walking—was in the area. When he saw Jesus, he fell at His feet and begged Him to come with Him to his house to heal his terminally ill daughter. Jesus was on His way to Jairus' house when His journey was interrupted by this next situation.

There was a woman that had an "issue of blood" (Mark 5:25 KJV). She was literally hemorrhaging daily. If that wasn't bad enough, this had been going on for twelve long years. What made it (her wilderness) worse was that she was in the worst state of loneliness. The Jewish laws said a person that had this type of issue could not go into the temple because of fear of contaminating others, and they were pronounced as unclean. The temple was the place of fellowship for all of them. So, she was isolated from friends, her community, family—everyone she loved. She had spent all she had going to doctors who had no cure for her. Poor, isolated, and lonely in her wilderness had been her existence for twelve long years. But she heard Jesus was in the area. She made up her mind, *I have been in the rear, isolated, without hope too long, and I'm going to press forward to see Jesus.*

Pressing past the traditions, the laws, the people (none of which could help her), she said, "If I just touch his clothes, I will be healed" (Mark 5:28 NIV). She did. And instantly, her hemorrhaging stopped. Jesus, even though the multitude of people surrounded him, asked who touched His clothes. Oh, it's so good to know one hand lifted in faith among millions of people can reach Jesus, get His attention, and receive what they need. She, trembling, admitted she was the one. He said, "Daughter, thy faith hath made thee whole; go in peace, and be whole of thy plague" (v. 31 KJV). She was not just *healed* but *whole*; she was to leave with "the peace...which passeth all understanding" (Philippians 4:7 KJV).

> *I dare you in the midst of your wilder-ness—no matter how long you have been there, and it appears that you will never come out—to continue to reach **out** and **up** in faith. You will find God's grace to help in your time of need and healing for your body, soul and mind.*

Meanwhile, Jairus is waiting. And during that wait, word is sent to him to trouble the Master no further, for his little daughter has died. This is the end. There was no *through this wilderness* and *but now it is over*. I can't imagine how he must have felt, but I'm sure his thoughts probably were something like this: *My daughter was dying; this woman had waited twelve years. One more day would not have mattered. She's going to live on, but my daughter, my little girl has died.* But little did Jairus know that his daughter had been upgraded from *sick* to *resurrected*.

You *might just be getting an upgrade for a greater miracle.*

Does your wilderness seem to be a place that you have now taken up residence, one of death and burial, a place you will never get out of? Your waiting on Jesus is never in vain.

The rest of the record tells us that Jesus told Jairus not to worry; that his daughter was not dead—just asleep. Jesus goes to Jairus' house, anyhow. Jairus' faith is depleted but not Jesus,' nor are His promises. Jesus puts out all the professional mourners that He finds there, even all of the disciples, except three, and commands they stop the music that accompanies their moaning and groaning. So, in the company of five people: the mother, father and three disciples (Peter, James, and John), Jesus simply says, "Little girl... arise" (v. 41), and she gets up, and He commands that her astonished parents give her something to eat. It is never too late; it is never hopeless as long as Jesus is in the house. No matter how long and how dismal things may look, just invite His presence. Welcome His presence and watch Him, along with the grace that He has promised, "do exceedingly abundantly above all that [you could] ask or think" (Ephesians 3:20).

CHAPTER 11

IN YOUR WILDERNESS YOU CAN BLOOM WHERE YOU HAVE BEEN PLANTED.

"The wilderness and the wasteland shall be glad for them, And the desert shall rejoice and blossom as the rose" (Isaiah 35:1).

The wilderness or the desert is a place that we expect to be absent of any greenery, vines that are flowing, or even grass. It's a place whose color, I feel, is the direct opposite of green. Brown is the new green in the desert because it's all around. It's dry for miles and miles; you see nothing but dirt and or sand. So, of course, it's not the place where you would even look for flowers to be blooming.

It was this desolate habitat that God had told His people (speaking of their future glory), that *the desert shall rejoice and blossom as the rose*. An impossibility—yes, with the natural eye, but with God, nothing is impossible. The most hopeless plant can be placed in an unproductive environment and bloom.

*You can bloom where **you** have been planted.*

With your eyes you cannot see it because the probability of one even surviving is next to nothing, let alone, blooming or flourishing. But here is where you start seeing things as God sees them, according to what He has promised. No matter where He has placed you and allowed you to be, you can blossom.

In the three chapters comprising the book of Habakkuk, the prophet (of the name of the book) was in such an emotional environment—a wilderness. After being there for a long time, he did not see any sign of God being on His people's side or that the promises He had given them would ever be fulfilled. The situation was that their enemy had triumphed over them. It appeared that God was not going to move and defeat their enemy as before, and that was final. Habakkuk, spokesperson for God, could not see any response or even share with the people a word of encouragement from God. This was a desolate state. Can you picture a tree standing in the middle of nowhere, displaying dry branches, with not even one solitary leaf? Just dry sticks protruding out from the trunk? You'd think the only thing that it could wait for was someone to cut it down because what use was it?

Naturally, before a tree produces fruit, there is a process. The branches produce the leaves; the bud for flowers shows up; and the gentle Spring rain feeds and encourages the blossom to open. The blossom is the sign that there will be fruit and later a harvest. But in this case, there were no conditions to show that there would be any such thing. You can imagine how Habakkuk was feeling. He was discouraged, so how could he encourage anyone?

There is a New Testament story (see Luke 13:6-9) that tells this parable:

> *A certain man had a fig tree planted in his vineyard, and he came [looking for] fruit on it and found none. Then he said to the keeper of his vineyard, 'Look, for*

> *three years I have come seeking fruit on*
> *this fig tree and find none. Cut it down.'*

It was standing but was not yielding its purpose. What was it good for? The owner said that it was just taking up room. Have you ever felt that way? Not seeing any fruit of your labor? In a barren place...just taking up room? The enemy (or it does not even have to be the enemy—just someone else prospering) not putting, it seems, any effort into what they are doing and just blooming, reaping harvest after harvest? Then you can identify with Habakkuk. But don't lose hope! God is not through with you yet; when it seems like there is no hope, there is always another chance.

Luke continues the parable of Jesus:

> *But he [the caretaker] answered and*
> *said to him, 'Sir, let it alone this year also,*
> *until I dig around it and fertilize it. And if*
> *it bears fruit, well. But if not, after that*
> *you can cut it down.'*

Habakkuk's physical *leaves* of expectation were, if you will, drooping. A second look would reveal no buds of hope showing. Maybe if there was some-thing—just a little something— that would show a possibility of change in this metamorphosis of his life... But God had called and placed him in this time period of Israel's life.

Could he bloom where God had planted him?

Water, of course, is what is needed in a desert, and God can certainly provide it. Had not the Psalmist promised that there is a river that flows from the throne of God? (See Psalm 46:4.) Yes, but where was it? Habakkuk knew God had called and placed him in this time period, and what He needed was a response from the Lord God who sees eternity past, present, and future. So, Habakkuk says: "I will stand my watch And set myself on the rampart, And watch to see what He will say to me" (Habakkuk 2:1).

So, he waits on the Lord; he rests in the Lord. He knows the Lord will speak.

He alone is God, who can never be sought in vain.
Saint Bernard of Clairvaux

And He does. The Lord says:

Write the vision, [He has given one]
And make it plain on tablets [remind yourself and...]
That he may run who reads it [inspire others] (v. 2)

Why can I?
For the vision is yet for an appointed time;
But at the end it will speak, and it will not lie.
Though it tarries, wait for it;
Because it will surely come,
It will not tarry. (v. 3)

We have become so accustomed to this hurried world that we've begun to demand speed in our spiritual life, too. However, God acts on behalf of those who wait for him. "Since ancient times no one has heard, no ear has perceived, no eye has seen any God besides you, who acts on behalf of those who wait for him" (Isaiah 64:4 NIV). Wise believers endure until the fruits of their labor appear.

Just because God is silent does not mean that He is not working on your behalf wherever you are planted. Your dream/vision are still active though you cannot see the performance. You will bloom where He has planted you, in His perfect timing. Your blossoming will be seen according to your obedience to what He says.

Here is the key that God tells Habakkuk: "The just shall live by his faith (Habakkuk 2:4).

And as we learn in the New Testament: "Faith is the substance of things hoped for, the evidence of things NOT Seen (Hebrews 11:1 emphasis added).

Habakkuk started seeing things as God sees them with the eyes of faith and started speaking in faith. The Hebrew word for faith here is *emunah* and it means *steadfastness or faithfulness.* Paul's words to the Corinthian church speak to us when we are in that place that is dismal, dry, and unproductive: "Be steadfast, immovable, always abounding in the work of the Lord, knowing that *YOUR* labor is not in vain in the Lord" (1 Corinthians 15:58 emphasis added). Stay there. You can and will bloom where you have been planted. He will supply what you need. He gives grace in your wilderness—sustaining, productive, unmeasurable, bountiful grace to fulfill your purpose.

Habakkuk's encouragement came not to try and see it first but to trust the God who had promised during this crucial time of his life.

The enemy will not go without punishment.

Now the God of eternity present and future speaks to His prophet, letting him know about the circumstances of their enemy and tells Habakkuk to deliver a message to His people. Here are the blossoms of purpose as God speaks to the prophet about the crimes of an evil nation.

Five woes are pronounced. (See Habakkuk 2:5-19 HBCS.) These warnings we need to pay heed to are just as timely today as they were then, and they are prophetically for all generations to come. All will ultimately answer to God for violating His commands.

1. *"Woe to him who increases what is not his"* (v. 6). When a nation grows wealthy through extortion, robbery, and plundering others as

Babylon was doing to Jerusalem at that time, God pronounces a judgment on them.

2. *"Woe to him who covets evil gain for his house"* (v. 9). When all that you are concerned about is **your** house or **your** possessions, you will do anything to maintain them, whether you are a person, a family, or a nation. Sometimes we deceive ourselves believing the end justifies the means.

3. *"Woe to him who builds a town with blood-shed"* (v. 12*)*. I think about gang-related crimes and the mafia of years ago (that even exist now), about drug wars and cartels shedding much innocent blood to attain personal gain. History repeats itself over and over as we list events of years past: North against the South bringing about the Civil War. Going back further in history, land taken away from the American Indians, shedding blood to achieve more territory. So many territorial boundaries that exist today that were obtained by bloodshed. When you stand for what is right, the righteousness of God supersedes any other circumstance, allegiance, or man-made laws.

(Terrence Russell, my son, added from his experiences):

Establishing an allegiance to the standards based upon GOD's righteousness and holiness will set precedence for you when problems or circumstances present themselves that cause others to react in a lawless manner. This foundation must be established beforehand so that the stability in taking a stand is a reflex and not a decision under duress. It also establishes credibility among others who, though choosing to react with practice of lawlessness, will, out of respect, not expect you to join them, no matter what your ties may be. (This is very evident when those circumstances involve territorial wars.) Our declaration of being men/women of God is not only verbal but also accompanied by action. This is how the Grace of GOD can be activated in the life of the believer when faced with temptation to follow laws or creeds contrary to the law of Righteousness. The standard of living established by the Righteousness of

GOD supersedes any laws, creeds, or popular majority decisions."

4. *"Woe to him who gives drink to is neighbor... that you may look on his nakedness!"* (v.15). A record of this happened in Genesis 9:21-25. Noah drank wine from his vineyard after the flood, got drunk and became uncovered and was exposed. His son, Ham, saw it and told his brothers, instead of covering him. His other sons would not look upon their father's nakedness (mocking him) but covered him up. When Noah awoke and heard what Ham had done, he cursed Canaan, who was the son of Ham, to be servants of servants. Proverbs 20:1 (KJV) reminds us that "wine is a mocker, [and] strong drink is raging." When you give alcohol to someone to expose them or use him or her for your purposes, God says, "Woe to you."

5. *"Woe to him who says to wood, 'Awake!'"* The Babylonians were idol worshipers and reaped God's judgment for worshiping them; many of the idols were made out of wood. Along with this worship, they practiced astrology and magic. Through generations, as it is even

today, men conducting their lives by astrology and witchcraft is prevailing.

Even now, God is looking for men and women to "cry aloud, [and] spare not" against the wickedness. Through the voice of Isaiah, He says, "Tell My people their transgression, And... their sins" (Isaiah 58:1). Your surrounding area where you have been planted may appear as if it is a dead, unproductive place, giving opportunity to change your focus to depend on other things, trying other methods to get away from there. You can be the example of light in that same place. God has planted you there, and when you have been planted, He expects you to bloom. And the blossoms of your purpose will be evident as He gives you grace in your wilderness.

Habakkuk saw firsthand the evil around him in epidemic form. He, at first, questioned God, but then he heard God's answers that He did not want His people (nation) to fall to the Babylonians, nor pick up their ways. Above all, he learned that the Lord was still in control of everything. In His timing, He sometimes will even use unexpected ways to accomplish His greater purpose.

So, it is plain what I am to do: Write the vision. The vision is your victory. Write it in faith; it will come to pass. Though it tarries—appears that *it* or *you* are there a long time waiting, waiting in vain—*it will surely come.*

Habakkuk bloomed where he was planted. He learned that sometimes when the situation seems out of the control of God, and you think He might have forgotten you in the place that you are in, the good news is that you can ask God questions, and God will answer.

The just lives by faith during the good times and the bad times, when it is easily seen, and, especially, when I can't. God is faithful. The end result was not that God showed up and answered (and He did), but the greater was that Habakkuk's focus was completely changed. It's not always about the end result that we so desired or a way out which we think is the victory. The wilderness is also a place of faith building.

Habakkuk spoke it himself, and this speaks to us when we find ourselves in those dry, unproductive places in our lives, our personal wilderness. When the *whys* of our lives that have no answers come and we just don't understand, we should remember, "The just shall live by his faith" (Habakkuk 2:4).

Habakkuk 3:17-19 is a hymn of Faith:

> *Though the fig tree may not blossom,*
> *Nor fruit be on the vines;*
> *Though the labor of the olive may fail,*
> *And the fields yield no food;*
> *Though the flock may be cut off*
> *from the fold,*
> *And there be no herd in the stalls—*
> *Yet I will rejoice in the Lord,*
> *I will joy in the God of my salvation.*
> *The Lord God is my strength;*
> *He will make my feet like deer's feet,*
> *And He will make me walk on my high hills.*

I am not moved by what I presently see; I stand in this security—God's Word that says what moves Him is Faith. "Without faith it is impossible to please him... He is a rewarder of those that diligently [and consistently] seek Him" (Hebrews 11:6), not looking for what our natural eyes see at the present time.

My natural eye sees the barren tree with no blossoms or fruit on the vines. My natural eye sees no immediate results from my laboring. The ultimate answer to all of our questions is to trust in God. When all of these things threaten us, we can trust that God still reigns and will work out His sovereign purpose for our good.

No blossoms? I can still bloom where He has planted me, stemming from my trust in Him, not in what I see.

Remember God told Habakkuk, "At the End it WILL speak and it [can] not lie" (Habakkuk 2:3 emphasis mine). Faith-filled waiting to bear fruit is needed. ***My blossoming comes from within.*** I bloom where I have been planted, waiting in exciting anticipation for the fruit that follows. God's memory is perfect. He is able to remember our prayers not only for years but also for generations beyond our lifetime.

Know when you are heard, you are healed.

He will restore the years, that the devourer has eaten up and taken away. (See Joel 2:23-26.)

God's timing is rarely our own, but it is always worth waiting for. While I'm waiting, He gives me joy so I can *rejoice.* Others will see me rejoicing, which is completely contrary to what is surrounding me. *I am blooming in this desert place.* My blossoming comes from within.

> *Therefore they shall come and sing in the height of Zion, and shall flow together to the goodness of the Lord, for wheat, and for wine, and for oil, and for the young of the flock and of the herd: and their soul shall be as a watered garden. (Jeremiah 31:12 KJV)*

Regardless of *how treacherous* the journey or *how bleak* the wilderness may seem, He gives us sure footing and enables us to dance on the heights.

Sure footing...*making my feet like deer's feet.*

Well, the Habakkuk 3: 19 Scripture says, "make my feet," which implies there has to be a change. A change God causes in my feet before I go to the next level. If I don't have sure footing, I can fall, or, in this case, my movement or climb is hindered, and the mountain that I'm climbing up can result in something very detrimental to my direction.

Feet: We all know the importance of feet; without them, there is no movement. In this situation, there can be no escalating us from this hopelessly desolated place (wilderness/valley).

I already have feet, but He makes them to adapt or become conducive for climbing for my purpose, as he uses deer feet for an example.

Those deer, I am told, that climb have special hoofs that are divided and will cling to the rocks as they go up. This sets them apart from other types.

*How will my feet change to move on to my purpose
and go up to the next level?*

I think of pedicures, which is the closest example
of a change in my feet. Pedicures are a pruning,
shaving, and cutting away of those things that hurt
and hinder our feet from doing what they are made
to do at their fullest potential. If I get them consistently, my feet look and feel better, and my shoes fit
better. Therefore traveling, I can do so without the
hindrances of calluses, corns, or any growths that
develop on my feet resulting from age or ill-fitting
shoes during this life's journey.

I saw this clearly and physically one evening after
a long flight from Chicago to Las Vegas. I had just had
a pedicure before I left. It was a special one with an
added process that I had never had before. When I
entered my hotel room and removed my socks, I dis-
covered there was dead skin—and not just a little
in a few areas. It was coming from all over my feet
and was falling off all over the place as I removed my
socks. This had never happened before. As I stroke my
feet, the dead skin just continued to fall off. I began
trying to think what might be causing this; but as it

came off so easily, and not remembering the special added process that the pedicurist had done, I saw a change in my feet. The color and new skin under the dead skin was that of a child (before calluses, corns, etc. invaded my feet).

The next thing I noticed was dead skin that was between my toes was coming out and off. I never thought about those places during a pedicure, having had many throughout the years or even when I attempted to do it myself. I started seeing that what was happening was the result of this new added process. It was a pruning, if you will.

Oh my! This was making my feet conducive to not only continue the journey but also accomplish a better journey and travel further. It was this new added special process that the pedicurist had done to my feet. It took a little longer in execution, but it was well worth the wait.

Sometimes, I believe this is what God does when it is needed for the next level of our journey's climb to higher heights. He prunes and clears away all the dead things in our lives so that we are not just enabled to continue our journey, but empowered to go up to those places that we have never been able to before without the excess baggage of hindrances to our climb to the next level that God wants us to go to.

Just as the promise, "If anyone is in Christ, he is a new creation; old things have passed away; behold, all things have become new" (1 Corinthians 5:17), it is manifested on this journey with Him. We have to lay aside all the weights that so easily hinder us from running this race. (See Hebrews 12:1.)

The wilderness can be a place of a pruning process. So, on the next journey with Him, we will have unloaded all the excess in the wilderness to move toward our destiny without hindrance. We can't do it ourselves (as my self-pedicures or any man-made process). Only God gets into the crevices, the unseen places, to remove the hindrance of the excess dead things in our lives—some we are not even aware of. *He **makes** my feet like deer's feet.* (See Habakkuk 3:19.)

CHAPTER 12

GROWING IN GRACE

"Therefore, dear friends, since you know this ..., be on your guard, so that you are not led [astray] ...and fall from your own stability. But grow in the grace and knowledge of our Lord and Savior Jesus Christ" (2 Peter 3:17,18 HCSB).

T **he im**possible has happened; I can bloom and **grow** in this wilderness. In fact, that is the measuring stick by which I will be able to exit. What was God trying to teach me and nurture me so I can grow thereby?

I have learned that once you have learned something through your experiences with God, it is something no one can take away from you. I call it a *deep place* in you, in your own personal knower. It's that seed that has been planted and watered and has taken root and now brings forth the fruit, in spite of the circumstances. You now **know** He can and will do what He promised.

In fact, no one thought you were going to survive. You were like that tree that was commanded to be cut down because its owner thought it was not good for anything because its purpose was not seen. (See Luke 13:6-9 KJV.) Yet, the keeper of the vineyard said, "Let it alone this year also, till I shall dig about it, [nourish it] and dung it" (v. 8). Dig around it so that the rain can penetrate into its dry soil better. Place in it whatever it needs to encourage growth—dung it. Dung it seems to me a last result, but not really; it's just a necessary nutrient. Dung as a nutrient?

Dung it—those stinky trials that you had to go through but were needed for your growth, for your good—to produce the harvest in your life.

For a tree to grow to its maximum and produce what it has been planted for, one thing that is added is dung. The smell and the idea are repulsive. How can anything like that be any good or good for any purpose? But God can take that which is awful, smelly, unwanted, to be nothing but cast aside, and use it for our good. *That's exactly what we were before Christ came into our lives.*

God uses trials (those smelly, despicable things) to make and mold us so that we will grow into the potential that only He knows we can be. Our finite minds cannot understand His methods or ways, but He is God, and He knows what He is doing.

Sufficient Grace

I thought the Christian life was going to be easier than this. Have these words ever entered your mind? Sometimes we come into the family of God thinking that our heavenly Father will fix all our problems and devote Himself to our happiness and comfort. However, that is not the reality portrayed in Scripture. (See 2 Corinthians 12:7-10.) Paul was a man whom the Lord used greatly, and yet his life was anything but easy. In fact, at one point, the apostle thought his pain was too much to bear, and he begged God to remove it. There's nothing wrong with asking the Lord to relieve our suffering, but what should our response be if He doesn't? Paul probably had no idea that his experience would find its way into our Bible to comfort and guide believers throughout the ages. The promise God gave him applies to us as well: "My grace is sufficient for you" (v. 9).

God's grace could be defined as His provision for us at the point of our need. The problem is that sometimes it doesn't seem as if the Lord truly is meeting our need. But He frequently sees deficiencies, outcomes, and complications that we don't. His goals for us involve spiritual growth, the development of Christlike character, and strong **faith**. And trials play a vital role in achieving these.

The important issue is, again, how we respond. If all you want is relief, you could descend into anger and doubt when that immediate relief does not happen. But if your desire is to become the person God wants you to be, you'll see each trial as an opportunity for Christ to display His character and strength in you. That is what we call growth. Not everything is centered around me, but it's about what He wants of me with His knowing the potential that is in me.

Growth says the following:

Yes Lord, I now know who I am and who I belong to, so mold me and make me after your will. I say yes, to whatever your plans are for me, I say yes, to the direction you want me to go in, even when it is entirely contrary to my goals and objectives. I can say yes now because the destiny that you have for me is far greater and better than I could ever realize for my own life. The reality of 'in everything give thanks' (1 Thes. 5:18) is foundational for my growth as the trials are the necessary fertilization.

I say yes. I am growing, growing in this knowledge. This knowledge, I have learned, will take me not only into places of heights and successes, but also into valleys and through wildernesses. But when I know Jesus, I can grow in the grace, the favor, which only He can give, supplying everything I need. I don't deserve this grace; yet He gives it to me, and it is unmeasurable. And in this knowledge, I'm learning more and more about Him who gives this grace: our Lord and Savior Jesus Christ.

You know, the more I know about Jesus, the more I want to know. The more I know, the more I love Him. I think about my first love. Do you remember yours? You wanted to spend time with them and express your love more to them. The time that you spent was never enough as you grew to know each other better and love them. In time, it became evidence that demanded a verdict. The verdict resulted in a commitment to marriage until death do us part.

That is just a smidgen as an example of the love that Jesus demonstrated for us. I think of His saving love for me, how He sacrificed everything, and knowing even if I was the only person on earth, He would still have come and died for me. He desires relationship with me, to be present with me all the time. Oh, what a love!

Knowing Him, learning more about Him—who is the Living Word—through the written word He left on record for us, we can see that He is the ultimate example for us. I see His valleys of despair, His mountain-top experiences with His Father, the victorious results that come from His relationship with His Father and His obedience, and the miracles He performed that He proclaimed we will do even greater things. (See John 14:12.) I learn and know that we can be "more than conquerors" (Romans 8:37) in every area of our lives.

Knowing Him and growing in the knowledge of Him.

The more I know about Him, the more I am encouraged to do those greater things that He says I can do through Him. And the possibilities in my life, I have learned, are innumerable and immeasurable. I am witnessing *the eyes have not seen nor ears heard things He has in store for me,* as referred to in 1 Corinthians 2:9.

I learned the words spoken, encompassing all the benefits, and now I know: "He was wounded for [my] transgressions...The chastisement for [my] peace was [laid] upon him, and [with those same] stripes, [I] am healed" (Isaiah 53:5). I am in possession of this truth—that whatever sickness comes upon me, I am healed—not later, but **now** because the price has already been paid for me. I can say it before the manifestation of it.

Growing in the knowledge of Him, I now say what He says and see it the way He sees it because He has proven himself to me over and over again. That peace that He purchased, I can have, even while I am going through my wilderness. I can go through with confidence because it is a peace that passes all understanding.

Even my enemies have no power over me because I have learned the power of forgiveness. When Jesus asked the Father to forgive those that did all the deplorable things to Him, He was able to say that they really don't know what they are doing. (See Luke 23:34.) For He knew His purpose, and anyone that fought Him was fighting against His purpose and did not have a clue that they would be found fighting against God, the Father. Therefore, I can also forgive whatever the situation or what anyone has done to me. I don't have to carry that burden, for I have learned that "when a man [or woman's] ways please the Lord, He makes even his enemies to be at peace with him" (Proverbs 16:7). And He makes them his footstool; a footstool: just an item or place that lifts you higher. (See Hebrews 1:13.)

When I feel that I am not capable of fulfilling those assignments for my life, He has told me, "I can do all things through him [Christ]" (Philippians 4:13

NIV). When I am at my wits' end thinking I can't go any further, He gives me that remarkable grace, and His "strength is made perfect in [my] weakness" (2 Corinthians 12:9), and I am able "to press toward the mark...of the high calling" (Philippians 3:14 KJV) in my life.

It's amazing that with this great knowledge, it lets me know I still don't know enough. I can echo Paul, "that I may know Him and the power of His resurrection, and the fellowship of His sufferings" (Philippians 3:10). Fellowship of His sufferings? Yes, because I am *shaped*: made into His image, character developed, anointing poured out upon me.

The intimacy that Paul desires and describes is one of a closeness that I desire more and more where nothing comes between my soul and my Savior. I am growing to be more like Jesus with no personal desire to be anything else. Paul says it like this, "I am crucified with Christ: nevertheless, I live; yet not I, but Christ liveth in me" (Galatians 2:20 KJV). And how powerful is the closing that Peter gives us? "But grow in grace and in the knowledge of our Lord and Savior Jesus Christ" (2 Peter 3:18 KJV).

Do you know this? Is this your desire? If so, your wilderness becomes a place of fellowship. You are not just alone, but alone in His presence—"the Author and Finisher of [your] faith" (Hebrews 12:2). Are you excited about the possibilities and the plans that He has for you and how this all is working and going to work together for your good? This *knowledge* settles our hearts and teaches us how to stand in every situation because He knows what He is doing.

However, the preceding verse in the instructions given by Peter that is referenced above gives a *warning*: Dear friends, since you know this in advance, be on your guard, so that you are not led away by the error of lawless people and fall from your own stability. I have to be on my guard when I have this knowledge because I can be led astray and fall from my own stability. When you think you stand, take heed lest you fall. (See 1 Corinthians 10:12.)

How can I be led astray and fall, if I know these truths?

Looking at this last letter that Peter writes to the church, it starts out by telling us the growth of true knowledge. Even knowledge grows; therefore, we can never stop learning and growing. And as we are building, we will know that we will never fall; that is the promise. Listen to how we build, or, as Peter uses the word, *add.*

> *And beside this, giving all diligence, add to your faith virtue; and to virtue knowledge; And to knowledge temperance; and to temperance patience; and to patience godliness; And to godliness brotherly kindness; and to brotherly kindness charity. For if these things be in you, and abound, they make you that ye shall neither be barren nor unfruitful in the knowledge of our Lord Jesus Christ. But he that lacketh these things is blind, and cannot see afar off, and hath forgotten that he was purged from his old sins. Wherefore the rather, brethren, give diligence to make your calling and election sure: for if ye do these things, ye shall never fall. (2 Peter 1:5-10)*

You will *never* fall. What a great promise! Peter continues to say, it's not enough to know but to constantly be put in remembrance of them. He says to *stir* (not allow this to settle as information only), "to stir you up by putting you in remembrance" (2 Peter 1:13 KJV).

Peter tells us the basis of true knowledge is Jesus Christ, who is truth. He told his listeners, "We have not followed cunningly devised fables...but were eyewitnesses of his majesty" (2 Peter 1:13 KJV). This is not all just a fairy tale or a fantasy to make you feel better, but it is truth, rooted and grounded in a person—Jesus Christ.

Further, Peter warns us in the next chapter, speaking from his experience, to alert us even for today. "There were false prophets also among the people, even as there shall be false teachers among you, who privily shall bring in damnable heresies, even denying the Lord that bought them [taking you away from truth], and bring upon themselves swift destruction. And many shall follow their pernicious ways" (2 Peter 2:1-2 KJV).

He describes these teachers as "wells without water, clouds that are carried with a tempest" (v.17).

They will "speak great swelling words of vanity [that] allure through the lusts of the flesh... They [will] promise...liberty, [and] they themselves are the servants of corruption" (vv. 18-19). How will we know them? They are overcome by the same corruption. How true we know this to be, as we see this happening over and over again today, even more than when this was written by Peter.

Peter goes on to speak of the *last days* in the next chapter with the coming of "scoffers, walking after their own lusts. They will even start denying that Jesus' promise of returning is true, since we have heard it for such a long time. He closes by addressing longevity and encouraging us. He said, "Beloved, be not ignorant of this one thing, that one day is with the Lord as a thousand years, and a thousand years as one day".

Whenever you are going through a wilderness, keep your focus. Remind yourself of the prophetic events that are happening and will happen. Know that Jesus is there with you and will supply all of your needs no matter what the circumstance, and ***His grace is sufficient***.

Most important than anything else, learn to look beyond the present circumstances but unto our soon coming King. It will be worth it all. The Lord is not slack concerning his promise, as some men count slackness. In this world of politics and political ambitions, when promises are broken as soon as they are made, know that there is One that can **not** lie. Heaven and earth will pass away before one jot or tittle of His word will fail.

CHAPTER 13

LEARNING HOW TO OPERATE IN GOD'S TIMING

Remember when we were talking about Habakkuk and how important time is?

Again, God's timing is rarely our own, but it is always worth waiting for.

Here is the question: How do I know what is God's timing?

*God **is** time **personified.***

Revelations 22:13 (KJV) reminds us what Jesus said: "I am Alpha and Omega, the beginning and the end." He started everything, and He is the ending and the sum total of it all. We are simply somewhere in the middle, waiting for His time to be manifested in our lives, or, as the Scripture "When the fullness of time was come…"

God does not operate on a time schedule, though He does everything "decently and in order" (1 Corinthians 14:40). He never looks at a watch to make sure He is *on time*. We often use the phrase, "He never comes when you want Him to, but He is always *on time*"; yet, His timing is always perfect.

One important thing we must learn is that while we have to wait, it does not mean He is denying us of what we asked for. In other words, God's **delay is not denial**; it's His perfect timing.

Daniel learned the process of delay.

Daniel had a vision that he said was true, but the time appointed was long. It was taking so long to manifest. He fasted and prayed to hear what the Lord had to say about it, desiring more than anything to get an understanding. After a period of time, the angel Michael, the warrior for God's people, showed up and explained the delay. Michael tells what happened: The moment Daniel had prayed, God had heard his request and sent the answer, but the enemy showed up and held up his request (delayed his answer for that time period). It was warfare in the heavenlies, a battle that had to be fought in order for his request/ prayer to be answered and received, or, in this case, released. His request was delayed—not denied. (See Daniel 10.)

This lets us know what happens when we pray. It is warfare. A battle goes on against the enemy that does not want us to receive what the Lord has promised, and we must fight to receive. This reminds us of what Jesus said, "The kingdom of heaven suffers violence, and the violent take it by force" (Matthew 11:12).

I have learned this: <u>the greater the blessing, the greater the battle</u>. We understand what is great about our battles. We physically do not have to fight because the battle belongs to the Lord. As in every battle, there is a need for weapons; however, the weapons that we use are not the natural ones of warfare, not carnal. They are spiritual weapons God supplies to us of which the greatest weapon is prayer.

We pray; He fights. We fast and His response, losing the bands of the wicked, setting the captive free. (See Isaiah 58:6.) However, even delays are still God's perfect timing, for God had purpose in it for

Daniel. Daniel had to learn (so we also) the process of delay: the warfare that goes on to release our answer, the discouragement that can happen but the consistency that we must prevail, *until*...

Jesus said to ask, seek, knock. He used the parable of the friend that had someone to visit his house unexpectantly at a very late hour, and he did not have any provisions for him or her. The visitor called out to him, but there was no answer because of the time of night it was. He kept on calling out to his friend because he knew that his friend had what he needed at that time. So, he persistently knocked on the door until his friend answered. (See Luke 11:5-13.)

What is the lesson Jesus was giving us? You ask; if there is no answer, seek. Seeking is not looking for the answer but seeking the God who has promised and who has the answer. Seek Him, the Problem-solver that you know beyond the shadow of a doubt has the answer. This confidence comes as you seek Him. Then, with this confidence, we can knock, and the door shall be opened. There was a time period when it was a delay (didn't get my answer right away), but it was not a denial.

Dear Reader, you may be experiencing a *night time* in your need. The darkness of no response seems to surround you—spreading, enveloping you. It appears as a darkness with no possible light of an acknowledgement or even an answer in view. The enemy is holding up what God has promised you.

But don't give up. Be persistent petitioning this Friend. Know that you are petitioning the "friend that sticks closer than [any] brother" (Proverbs 18:24), and this Friend has all that you need and will supply all. Keep asking, seeking, knocking. It is just a delay, not a denial. God has a perfect timing for you. It's called your personal *appointed time*. He orchestrates everything that's necessary for you to receive, pulling it all together as a conductor directs each instrument in an orchestra, synchronizing them until it all sounds like one beautiful sound. The Bible calls it "the fullness of time" (Galatians 4:4 ESV). The enemy's job is to get you discouraged and to have you give up in this time and place of wilderness in your life. God's timing will be the best time. I repeat; *God's timing will be your best time*. Learn how to operate in His time using what He has provided for you.

Daniel had prayed for an understanding, but little did he know the extent of what God had in store for him and was going to entrust him with. In this, God's perfect timing was to reveal to Daniel in his vision, not just what was happening in his present time but also for the entire prophetic end times that generations to come would need to know. No wonder the enemy *tried* to delay this...

This does not negate that God is our present help in the time of trouble. He is always there whether we feel it or don't even realize it. He sometimes answers before we even call, and the glorious times of when we are still speaking about it, He gives and we see the answer. (See Isaiah 65:24.) But also, we need to understand that although it seems like a delay, God is doing a greater work in us in preparation to receive what He is entrusting us to do for Him that He will be glorified.

CHAPTER 14

WHEN GRACE HAS BEEN LIFTED...

Every dead end is a destiny waiting to begin.

You have been on this mountain long enough.
It's time...

T he people of God had been in the wilderness for 40 years, and God had been their present help, provider and whatever they needed. He extended grace in the wilderness in spite of their consistent disobedience. That wonderful, unmerited favor He supplies, they experienced it over and over. A new generation was born, and God's promise was not to fail. It was time for them to leave that place.

The old generation had died out, and only the ones that had trusted God during this time and believed that God could do anything, even after such a long time, would leave that place. It was they who were getting ready to inherit that land of promise.

Sometimes our wilderness experience is for us to die to some of the things in our lives so that we will not carry any baggage with us into that place God is taking us. It's the purging of the dross that hangs on to us that keeps us from coming forth as *pure gold*. It's the doubt that plagues us. Sometimes it's the inconsistency of our emotions from mountain-top belief to valley discouragement. It's the time element: *Will He ever do what He promised*? It's the weariness that we experience in well doing and not seeing results.

From the account recorded in the 13th and 14th chapter of Numbers, I can imagine Joshua and Caleb saying, "No matter what our eyes see, our God is greater, and whatever we need, He will supply. We can go forward."

Whatever place God allows us to be in, we can bloom. We can "prosper...and be in health, just as [our] soul prospers" (3 John 1:2). Our spirit, that part of us that communicates with God, is growing larger than the flesh man. It is the flesh that the enemy consistently tries to feed, infiltrating our minds and thought process with doubt, discouragement, and depression. I now come to know that in this place walks the "Greater is He that is in [me], than he that is in the world" (1 John 4:4 KJV). The wilderness place prepared me for the promises that God gave me. The wilderness strengthens me, and the same God that took me through, providing everything I need will do the same for you. Grace is now being lifted for this place.

When it is time to move on.

Exiting the Wilderness

God has supplied grace in the wilderness and all of the benefits that it affords us. From this experience, coupled with this infusion, we experience growth, direction, and character building. Grace, that *amazing grace* that brought me safe thus far is the grace that will lead me home. Home is the place of promise. Amazing grace really has no description, and no language can define or express it. What I do know is I **didn't** and **don't** deserve it. It is what my Father used to save me when I was lost. It took the blinders off my eyes, and now I can see the life that is greater than anything that I could hope for. It gave me the eyes to see a life that is far beyond and much better than I ever anticipated. This is what I call the eternal grace. I stop to think about the measure of grace that He supplies in my wilderness which brings the question: *If grace is supplied in this wilderness for this time, when do we know it is time to move on*? I found that it is signaled again by that amazing grace. <u>This grace is now lifting</u>.

Satisfied with the necessities or walking in the Promises.

All that was needed in the wilderness was supplied.

When God's people walked through their wilderness, they were supplied with the necessities of life because God promised to supply all of their needs. They had manna and quail for food, as well as the same clothing that never wore out. But a change has to come. It was time to go into the promised land. It was time to exit the wilderness. Changes come when grace has been lifted.

There would be **No more manna** raining from heaven daily. Now they would have to walk into promises where the land would produce—the land flowing with milk and honey; the land where God said that every place they set their foot would be theirs. (See Joshua 1:3.) No more sojourners would they be traveling through, renting or leasing land that was not theirs. This land of promise would belong to them. <u>They were coming out of this wilderness into the great promises that the wilderness experience had been getting</u> them ready for.

However, there can be times when we get so accustomed to our wilderness that we don't want to move on. Just the manna and quail now and then and water as needed would be okay. We can become stationary and satisfied but living beneath our privilege and what has been promised when it's time to move on.

We set up residence as did the 2½ tribes out of the twelve that asked to stay on the other side of the river and not go into the promised land. We are comfortable here; this place meets our needs. Why should we go any further?

If you do not see now what has been promised, what you saw before, don't unpack your bags there. — Bishop Carl Pierce, Sr. sermon

Settling for less, we start complaining and actually fearing the promises, as demonstrated by what the people did when Moses sent the twelve spies into the promised land. (See Numbers 13.) They were sent to observe how the land was being inhabited before the Israelites were to go in to possess it. Two came back with a report of blessings far more than what they had imagined. The other ten saw only the giants that lived there. How foolish that report was when God had taken them through their wilderness and fought their battles, and they had become more than conquerors, in spite of themselves.

We, today, have been promised that we are overcomers. Jesus gave us the great promise: "Be of good cheer, [for] I have overcome the world" (John 16:33.) Since He has overcome the world, there is nothing in this world that we cannot overcome. It was not just a statement. After the crucifixion, He said, "It is finished!" (John 19:30). By His death, He overcame death when He rose from the grave three days later. He overcame the last stronghold over humanity and everything that confronts us. It has already been done. Therefore, I am an overcomer **before** the situation presents itself to me.

But in the case of the Israelites, and many times with us, fear caused them to see giants and not blessings, eradicating in their minds God's afore stated promises. When you start seeing the **problems bigger than the promise**, it will cause you to fear and retreat instead of going forward to claim your promise. Fear will cause you to build a house (a permanent dwelling place in your wilderness) when you are supposed to just pass through. It is fear causing you not to take the next step. This fear is of the devil.

It could be fear of the unknown, even when God said, "The steps of a good man are ordered by the Lord, And He delights in his way" (Psalms. 37:23).

"Haven't I commanded you: be strong and courageous? Do not be afraid or discouraged, for the Lord your God is with you wherever you go" (Joshua 1:9 HCSB.) These words that God spoke to Joshua over 3,000 years ago are very much on target for us today.

*There is only one fear that we are to have,
and that is the fear of the Lord, which is
a reverential fear.*

The psalmist said, "The fear of the Lord is pure, enduring forever. [It makes me want to obey his word regardless of the circumstances [because] the ordinances of the Lord are reliable and altogether righteous. They are more desirable than gold—than an abundance of pure gold; and sweeter than honey, which comes from the honeycomb" (Psalms.19:9-10 HCSB).

For the Israelites, was this not that land that was promised to flow with milk and honey? This was a direct blessing of the favor and provision of God for the desires of their heart. This was more than simply supplying all of their needs. God is challenging us and reminding us: *This is your time and season to walk into your promises that are far greater than what you could ask or think.*

Grace is lifting.

The grace of provision, favor, and peace found in the wilderness is lifting because it is time to move forward. The grace for your wilderness experience is leaving because it's time for you to leave, to move on. There is something greater. This was just a season, not a habitation. The season was great, and you saw the hand of God in providing and His promise fulfilled: "I will even make a way in the wilderness, and rivers in the desert" (Isaiah 43:19 KJV). However, the promise extends further than the present time. That was great, but there was also a promise to generations past that would be fulfilled in this present time.

> *For I will pour water upon him that is thirsty, and floods upon the dry ground: I will pour my spirit upon thy seed, and my blessing upon thine offspring. (Isaiah 44:3)*

I will pour water.

Water is life. Anything that is dry—even almost dead—water will revive. Pouring water on a plant will bring it back to life. Water transforms from death to life. This is not simply having a drink of water but *pouring water* on that need upon *him that is thirsty.*

Moving further, the promise is that water will also saturate your environment, everything around you— extending the blessings upon your children and offspring.

You may feel that the Lord is now saying: "You have been here long enough. You have learned what I wanted you to learn. Your need for this place has been met and it's time to move forward." So, what God does is start lifting the grace that He gave you for that place, time, and season. You, perhaps, feel the anxiousness that you never felt before; you feel the *sense of over* or incompleteness that God is not through. At some point, you may have a feeling of over anxiousness. This is not an anxiety attack; this is God pushing you "toward the mark...of the high calling" (Philippians 3:14 KJV). Perhaps another door is opening for ministry, a door that I have not been accustomed to, one that is different from what I have ever experienced.

Important: It does not have to be a geographical move but another level. Careful! this time can be one of the greatest deceptions. We can think it is geo- graphical and move into another location, and the end result can be running from place to place. When you are in this place, make sure you hear the voice of the Lord, not *the circumstances of the environment.*

Sometimes, I see that I am experiencing a greater anointing than I have experienced before because the promise that I have received is going to need this level of anointing. The olives have been crushed in the wilderness, and the oil of the anointing is flowing for this new season.

No more mana. As they proceed into the promise land, the manna stops.

Your manna of provisions while you were going through your situation ceases. We start desiring *more than*. It's not that we don't appreciated our daily needs being supplied, but it's time to move forward. This can be the start of a feeling of incompleteness even though I know God is more than enough, but He has promised to complete those things which concern me. (See Psalms.138:8.) Desiring more of Him and what goes along with that is Him revealing more to us. There is more. It's time now for the promises to unfold, in the land of promise. But there's one more river to cross, and for them, it's called *Jordan.*

CHAPTER 15

THE DEAD END
THAT IS DESTINY
WAITING TO HAPPEN

One more river to cross...to get to the promise.

In the past crossing, 40 years ago, the Israelites had passed through the Red Sea by God's marvelous intervention. God told Moses to stretch out his staff, and the river parted, and His people were able to cross over to get to their wilderness, their enemy drowning in the process. (See Exodus 14:31.) Now it was time to leave the wilderness and go into the Promised Land. But there was an obstacle called the Jordan River. Can you imagine those at the banks singing that old song, "So high you can't get over it; so wide you can't get around it...You must come in at the door"? Nice song, but... I *don't see a door.*

Fast forwarding about 1,400 years, Jesus would say, "I am the door" (John 10:7).

> *"The one who enters by the door is the shepherd of the sheep. The doorkeeper opens it for him, and the sheep hear his voice. He calls his own sheep by name and leads them out. When he has brought all his own outside, he goes ahead of them. The sheep follow him because they recognize his voice" (John 10:2-4 HCSB).*

At the Jordan River, Joshua is the new leader. His name means *The Lord will save* or *the Lord is Salvation*. Joshua, which is related to the name *Jesus*, takes his place giving instructions as follows. This time, the ark of the covenant, representing the presence of God, is to be lifted up by the priests, who are to walk first and then the people are to follow. Joshua gives different instructions from his predecessor, Moses.

Never be afraid to step out of the box of familiarity.

Joshua's instructions continue: "When the feet of the priests...rest in the Jordan's waters, its waters will be cut off. The water flowing downstream will stand up in a mass" (Joshua 3:13 HCSB).

You have entered a new season called *wilderness leaving*. You need to know the voice of the Lord and listen closely to His instructions: "My sheep hear my voice...and they follow me" (John 10:27). Your Jordan will be just another miracle. *Glory!* He has already gone before you making the way, and, sometimes, you will witness Him making ways out of no way.

They camped on the other side on the plains of Jericho. They observed the Passover. This was the feast that celebrates how death had passed over their house when God delivered them out of Egypt. (See Exodus 12.)

Guidance was provided from the wilderness into the Promised Land. Arriving there is an important moment in their history because this is the land God had promised to their ancestors. The conquest of this land occurred after the Israelites were attacked. They had to fight for what they knew God had promised them generations earlier. Why? because the Canaanites occupied the land, and they (the Israelites) now have to *possess* it.

Your promises have been placed before you, sealed by prayer, watered daily with the confidence that He cannot lie. You've been resting in the God that never fails, but it's not time to become sedentary, now that you are out of the wilderness.

They had to possess what the enemy occupied.

The enemy occupies, and, now, we have to possess that which God has already given to us. There would be giants in that land that the spies had testified about. But God had spoken to them; He would fight their enemies for them because their enemies would be His enemies.

However, God had also told them that He would not defeat their enemy all at once. Most times, we want the *all-at-once miracle,* not knowing the process God is working for us. Some delays in the journey have been the saving of your life. Some detours that you were complaining about taking you the long way have snatched you from harm's way because the enemy had laid a trap for you. **Always trust the process**.

God is in the business of using your enemies for your good. Just like Paul finally accepted when the thorn would not be removed from his side, he found that God's *grace was sufficient*. Now, with the Israelites, grace—the favor of God—would be demonstrated again as He went before them to do what they could not do. Not only were there giants in the land, but also lions. The Israelites did not know how to fight the lions, but the giants did. God would use their enemies to do what they could not do. Our enemy has been described as a roaring lion, walking to and fro seeking who he can devour but our God and Savior, Jesus Christ is also titled, the Lion of Judah. Who can stand before us when we call on that great name, Jesus, precious Jesus, we have the victory. Therefore, during this time, just continue to follow His guidance step by step, and experience each step as a miracle. You never have to fear your enemies; God's already got a plan for them, and it's for your good.

Grace lifted in the wilderness but was provided and flourishing again in the Promised Land. They could enter with a jubilant heart because He had brought them through a wilderness, not to leave them. We, too, should be excited about how He is going to continue this journey with us, knowing in Him we are always victorious. We should have a different mindset: *It already belongs to me, so the battle belongs to God. We are already victorious because He said that every place, I put my foot belongs to me. Joshua 1*

The wilderness place prepared me for the Promised Land.

That phrase is a great statement to repeat and to declare in your life. Say it to yourself as you start walking in the promise. "The wilderness place strengthened me, and the same God that allowed me to go through it will give me the grace, providing everything I need accompanied by His favor as I continue." As we walk to possess *our* promises, He will supply the weapons for our warfare to possess the land. Those weapons are "mighty through God...pulling down [the] strongholds" (2 Corinthians 10:4 KJV.) This was demonstrated when the Israelites encountered the walls of Jericho that fell down with the walk of faith and a shout. (See Joshua 6:20.)

Remember what He had spoken to them about walls?

Physical walls were built for protection and what were depended upon. The Israelites had learned that as strong as their city's walls were, those walls would not make them secure, and it was the same for the enemy's walls. The Spirit of the Living God would be their Defender. Since the walls that the inhabitants of Jericho had built could keep their enemies out due to the strength of their walls, they thought it would keep God's people from possessing the promises that God had made them. Jericho's ruins served as a reminder: It's "not by might nor by power, but by My Spirit, says the Lord" (Zechariah 4:6).

"The just shall live by faith" (Hebrews 10:38). God goes *before* me in every situation, defeating my enemies.

Back to the crossing. After the crossing, they celebrated:

While the Israelites camped at Gilgal on the plains of Jericho, they kept the Passover on the evening of the fourteenth

day of the month. The day after Passover
they ate unleavened bread and roasted
grain from the produce of the land. And
the day after they ate from the produce of
the land, the manna ceased. Since there
was no more manna for the Israelites,
they ate from the crops of the land of
Canaan that year. (Joshua 5:10-12 HCSB)

No more manna. Is that a feeling of sorrow or regret? God was providing greater things through His promised land, as they ate from the crops of the land of Canaan. It was the land where their enemy lived. The promise that He would "prepare a table before [them] in the presence of [their] enemies" (Psalms. 23:5) is manifested. <u>Always remember His promises when the enemy faces you with his threats.</u>

The table that He prepares is not a drive-through, pick-up, fast-food, eating-on-the-run place. When God prepares a table, it has chairs. You sit down, you rest, and you enjoy the food. Your enemy, many times, is the waiter that serves you because God prepares the table and uses whomever He wants. They are subject to you and what you want. He uses your enemy now to work on your behalf. Now, that is real rest, while it is all worked out.

> *Thus saith the Lord, The people which were left of the sword found grace in the wilderness; even Israel, when I went to cause him to rest. (Jeremiah 31:2 KJV)*

In this new place after crossing over from their wilderness, there is a variety of food. Though I am thankful for what He has provided in the past, I never settle for less. I was not there to stay. God had promised to meet my needs but is moving me forward to the best. Grace has lifted for you in the wilderness for you to move to the next season of the best.

Isaiah, the prophet, spoke in this season of wilderness, and we find it to be true because God wants to do and is doing a new thing in our lives:

> *Behold, I will do a new thing,*
> *Now it shall spring forth;*
> *Shall you not know it?*
> *I will even make a road in the wilderness*
> *And rivers in the desert. (Isaiah 43:19)*

Every dead end is a destiny waiting to begin.

He said He would. He does it. And He will do it again. The God of impossibility will open up heaven for His children and pour out blessings in the most dire, unproductive wastelands of life.

Does it seem like you are now at a dead end? It's the wilderness ending and where destiny begins. Not to worry. There is always sufficient grace for the next level. Excited? This new generation walks into the promises of God. The ones that dare to believe Him and not doubt are walking with them. They are looking back at all of Egypt's restrictions on them as slaves; on the boundaries and unproductiveness of a wilderness; and on living a life as a nomad and a wanderer.

Now, I plant my feet in the *right now* of my life. In fact, every place I place my feet, it's mine, according to the promise of God as I walk in the direction that He leads me for my life. I walk in confidence. I see the prayers being answered, doors opening that no man can shut, and blessings overtaking me. Over my enemies, I am the head because he (the devil) is under my feet. I am not running from him any longer (as

God promised when His people faced the miracle of the Red Sea). I will not see this enemy of my past any longer.

I press toward the mark of a higher calling, forgetting those things which are behind. My past will not dictate my future. The promise now is that every enemy from this time on is a defeated foe. I walk in victory. There will be enemies, but God said they are already defeated if I walk with Him. And "no weapon formed against [me] shall prosper" (Isaiah 54:17). I make a choice: "As for me and my house, we will serve the Lord" (Joshua 24:15). It was grace that brought me safe thus far, and grace will lead me on and throughout my journey.

CHAPTER 16

THAT MARVELOUS FAVOR OF GOD

We rely on Christ for our salvation, which is by grace, but, sometimes, try to go solo after that. If God's powerful, unmerited favor called *grace* was needed to save us, then we definitely also need it for the rest of our lives. Understand, we cannot live this life successfully without Him and the grace that He supplies. He supplies it without measure for each season, situation, and trial of our lives.

Nothing can overpower you. When the trials of life confront you, your soul is in anguish overshadowing the promises of God. God knows all about it. It did not catch Him by surprise. Stop and rest in Him. Be still and know that He is God and has allowed the situation to perfect you. Are you resting in the grace He is supplying?

Picture yourself lying back with a medical line in your arm, if you will, connecting to an IV of His grace flowing freely, sourcing from heaven's unlimited supply. It's the intensive care of your soul. I am spending that time with Him daily, and through a continuous infusion of His sustaining power, I can live a victorious life no matter where I find myself. Yes, He is the source, but greater than that, it's a personal relationship that I have established with Him—just me and my Savior, allowing nothing to come in between.

It's crawling up into the lap of Papa God and feeling the warmth of His arms embracing me as I lie comfortably and confidently against His chest. It's the greatest position in the world. No matter what other place I find myself in, I know I can trust Him. I am acknowledging that I am weak, but He is the strength of my life.

Labor and Rest.

It is here that I have answered His call and embraced His admonition: "Come unto me, all ye that labor and are heavy laden, and I will give you rest. Take my yoke upon you, and learn of me... For my yoke is easy, and my burden is light" (Matthew 11:28-30). I release that which has cumbered me about— the cares and problems in this life we are constantly trying to fix, spending a multitude of hours, only to find out there are never enough hours in the day. Yet, time is in His hands.

It is here that I cease from laboring, releasing the heaviness of burdens and giving them all to Him. It is there that He speaks to me and says:

> *Rest in Me. I have the solution, and I can work out in a few hours what will take you all day, and some have taken years, and it still has not worked out! Stop spending time on it and spend time with Me. Stop trying to figure it out and let Me work it out. There will be yokes, but doing it My way, the yoke is easy. There are burdens, but release them, and you will see I am the one that carries them, and, therefore, they are light.*

Cannot close this book without reiterating our responsibility.

When we trust Christ as our Savior and accept by faith what He did on the cross for us, by grace, we are saved. Therefore, we are always under the covering and covenant of God's grace and love. Nothing we can ever do can change that. "Where sin abounded, grace did much more abound" (Romans. 5:20); however, it is not grace that we should ever take for granted, to be trampled upon.

Grace is favor. The fullness of His blessings is the favor of God. We have a part as partakers of this grace; and being a partaker, we receive the fullness of His blessings. We need to remember, at the same time, our behavior and heart condition do determine whether we receive the fullness of His blessings.

Because God looks at our heart before anything else, the heart condition is so important. He "resists the proud but gives grace to the humble" (1 Peter 5:5). The Bible says He desires that we have a contrite heart and a humble spirit. For this to happen, all aspects of our lives must be surrendered to Jesus. Total surrender of our lives is saying He is Lord over our lives and gives Him the place to operate fully without any hindrance, and according to His will. We all desire God's favor, but are we willing to surrender all to receive it?

<u>Final Questions and Thought</u>

1. Are you living in a manner that positions you to receive His full blessings?
2. Have you surrendered your home, work place, work ethics, finances, health, and all relationships to Jesus Christ?

Prayerfully consider whether you have submitted all areas of your life. Recognize His authority in all things. Fully surrender by confessing:

- I walk in grace daily and as He promised.
- "Surely goodness and mercy shall follow me all the days of my life" (Psalms. 23:6).
- "The blessing of the Lord, it maketh [continually] rich, and he addeth no sorrow with it." (Proverbs 10:22 KJV)

Maranatha

BIBLIOGRAPHY

Bishop Carl Pierce, Sr. n.d. "Sermon from Carter Memorial Church Of God In Christ."

Chambers, Oswald. n.d. "My Utmost for His Highest: Updated Edition Hardcover – January 1, 1992." By Oswald Chambers.

Clairvaux), Saint Bernard (of. 1908. "Saint Bernard On Consideration – Saint Bernard (of Clairvaux)." Clarendon Press.

—. 1881. Saint Bernard on the Love of God. Kegan Paul.

Douroux, Margaret J. 1980. "If It Had Not Been for the Lord."

Nelson, Eds. Thomas. 2014. "The Modern Life Study Bible." By Eds. Thomas Nelson. Nelson, Thomas, Inc.

Stanley, Dr. Charles. n.d. "In Touch Ministry Sermon on Obedience and disobedience."

All Scriptures unless indicated are taken from New King James Version (NKJV)

Additional Bible Version References:

- AMP – Amplified Bible
- ESV – English Standard Version
- HCSB – Holman Christian Standard Bible
- KJV – King James Version
- NIV – New International Version
- NLT – New Living Translation

CPSIA information can be obtained
at www.ICGtesting.com
Printed in the USA
BVHW081817200421
605388BV00005B/553

9 781662 803581